PAOLO TULLIO
COOKS
ITALIAN

BLACKWATER PR...

Blackwater Press Ltd
1–5 North Frederick Street
Dublin 1

jloconnor@eircom.net

AN
641.594

ISBN 978-0-9563541-8-1

Printed in the Republic of Ireland.

Acknowledgements

Thanks to Terry Kavanagh, Roundwood's butcher, who supplied the meat for the photography.

Contents

To my mother Irene,
who taught me how to cook

Introduction

Every region of Italy, and there are 20 of them, has its own canon of gastronomy, and in 2009 an Italian publishing house brought out a weighty tome for each region's cuisine. This book does not attempt to be encyclopaedic. These are my favourite recipes, the dishes my mother and grandmother taught me from my region of Italy, Lazio. More importantly, they're all recipes that can be made with ingredients that are readily available in Ireland.

Cooking the Italian way is more of a mindset than the simple following of directions. Once you're clear in your mind that food is an important part of cultured living, once you realise it is better to live to eat than to eat to live, then you're already on the right path. Spend more time sourcing the very best of ingredients than you do preparing them, insist on the freshest foods, the ripest fruits and meats that come from traceable sources.

Food, its preparation and its consumption are integral to Italian life. It's woven into the very fabric of social interactions, it keeps families together and binds friendships. But to understand the Italian kitchen, you need to understand a little of the Italian mentality. Italy is a country of extremes, of passion and noise. Look around you on any busy street in Italy and you're watching street theatre. Interactions between people seem almost theatrical in their performance, the gestures are large, the voices are raised and yet this is no more than a simple conversation.

On the streets of Naples, this is taken a step further – the decibel level is higher, the concentration of humanity is denser, the chaos is palpable. In the old city, along the length of Via Spaccanapoli, the road is narrow, the windows face each other across no more than 3 metres, the street vendors shout their wares and the householders lower baskets on ropes from the upper stories to the street, where the vendors pack it with goods, take out the money and put in the change, and the basket is raised again. It's a scene unchanged for centuries, a scene that could easily be found in a bazaar or a souk.

There are things that Italians are more passionate about than others, and one of these is food. Most large towns have a daily market where you can buy many things like knock-off designer clothes and leather goods, shoes and household items, but mostly the market is for food. There will be stall after stall of cheeses, cured meats, fruit, vegetables, olives of every sort, herbs and chillies. In Italy, freshness is valued when it comes to food, so buying it daily is the norm.

Just like in France, every town, no matter how small, will have a bakery. Italian bread has the same property as French bread, it goes hard very quickly. The sort of bread we have here in Ireland that goes mouldy before it goes hard is unknown. So bread is bought daily, and often twice daily. We understand the concept of a bakery that distributes its breads over a 80-kilometre radius with a fleet of vans. On the Continent, that's virtually unknown. There, you buy your bread from your local bakery and you buy it fresh.

This obsession with fresh produce is a major part of Italian cookery. Even today, in a world of fast food and convenience food, Italians still prefer to take no short cuts. I know no Italian who doesn't prefer homemade pasta to shop bought. It's ingrained in the psyche, good food doesn't happen easily. So remember rule one of Italian cooking, it's always better if it's hard to do.

There's another major difference in the Italian approach to food, and that's the concept of the larder. The larder could be a room in a big house, preferably one that's cool, it may be simply a walk-in cupboard, or in apartments, just a press in the kitchen. But whatever the size, the larder is where you keep your dry goods, foods that don't need refrigeration and that will form the basis of meals. Hospitality is such an engrained part of Mediterranean life that not being able to offer a surprise guest something to eat would be seen by most Italians as a *brutta figura*, which you could translate as a loss of face. In short, it would be embarrassing, so the larder is there to ensure that whatever happens, there will never be a shortage of food.

Many traditional Italian foods were created to store gluts. The pigs were slaughtered in winter, and like the tomatoes in summer, there was more than could be eaten at once. The meat needed to be preserved, so the two back legs were salted and became prosciutto, the belly and sides were made into a kind of bacon called pancetta and the rest was chopped up and made into sausages, using the pig's own digestive gut as the casing. In this case, the sausages and the salamis were salted and air-dried, which was the only way to preserve meat before the advent of the refrigerator. Prosciutto and sausages are not difficult to make, and later in the book I'll take you through the process step by step.

The main principle in creating your larder is that whatever keeps should be made in a large quantity at one time and then stored for later use. Spending a day making enough tomato sauce for the year is actually less time consuming than making a small amount every day. It saves time in the long run and you eat better. The other point to remember is that there are no short cuts; the preparation is labour intensive and takes time, but if you care about how you eat, it's worth it.

In more traditional houses, the larder serves another purpose – it's where you store seasonal gluts. When I was a child, my grandmother would harvest her tomatoes in late July. There would be far more tomatoes than anyone could eat in a month, so they needed to be stored for the rest of the year. The family would gather in the *aia*, an open, paved area outside the house, and huge cauldrons of tomatoes would be placed on trivets and log fires lit underneath. The tomatoes were boiled and then they were bottled.

You might think that wide, open-topped jars would be perfect for tomatoes, and probably they would have been, but in the rural Italy of the 1950s, nothing was wasted. Everything was recycled and no one would have even considered buying preserving jars. You used what you had, and what Grandma had was beer bottles, the kind that took a crown cap. A beer bottle has an opening about the size of my little finger, so everyone in the family was handed a small stick, which was used to push the tomatoes into the bottle. It was messy and tedious work, but when it was done there were enough bottled tomatoes to last Grandma's household for a year.

Although much of what is prepared in Italian kitchens is labour intensive, it is very rarely complex. What is appreciated is the quality of the raw ingredients and the skilful use of flavour. Mixed herbs are not to be found in little jars in Italian supermarkets, a reflection of the fact that Italians like flavours that are clearly defined. Using too many flavours is like mixing too many colours together – you get muddy brown. The best example that I can think of that embodies the careful use of flavours is gremolata, the traditional accompaniment to osso buco. Combine chopped parsley, garlic and grated lemon rind in equal quantities and you end up with a taste that is greater than its parts; it makes a new flavour entirely, just as a painter mixing blue and yellow makes a new colour.

Throughout this book I have concentrated on clear, precise flavours. You'll be amazed how few flavours you need to make food taste good – sometimes salt and pepper are all you need. Be confident, be sparing with your flavours and you'll have mastered a major part of Italian cookery.

Despite being home to the Vatican, Italy is surprisingly secular. Of course, due deference is paid to the Church's heritage, but an outside observer would probably conclude that the state religion was gastronomy. Italians are obsessive about their food, they talk about it a lot, they plan meals endlessly, their newspapers and magazines are filled with tips and hints for cooking better. But most of all, they eat in groups. Sometimes it will be a large family group of three generations sitting around a big table and sometimes it will be a big group of friends. Meals make the glue that binds Italian society together.

Until recently, much of Italy's population was rural. It's a curious fact that almost all of the Italian peninsula is mountainous – the average width of the coastal strip is just six miles before the mountains begin. So unless your home was in the Po Valley in the north of Italy, you would live and work in the mountains. That defines much of what can be grown and defines the agriculture of a very large proportion of the Italian mainland. Making a living from mountain land isn't easy and the hardships of a rural economy based on agriculture are still firmly rooted in the memories of many Italians. They use the words *la miseria*, the misery, to describe the days of hardship and want. If you need a reason as to why Italians are so keen on excessively large meals, look no further than the racial memory of hunger.

In my lifetime, I've seen huge changes. For example, when I was a boy, the bread of the poor was maize bread. Maize grows well in Italy and produces large crops per hectare, so maize grain was cheap and hence maize bread was cheap. In the affluent society of today's Italy you can still find maize bread, but only in high-end restaurants and gourmet shops. You won't find it on the table of the average household because it still carries the stigma of poverty.

There are parallels with Ireland here. Where do you find the dishes that your grandparents ate, like offal, crubeens and rabbit? Only in top-end restaurants, where you pay handsomely for the privilege. Memories of poorer times still make these foods difficult to eat.

Yet it's precisely the simplicity of these foods that is the basis of much of Italy's regional cooking. What we call peasant food is no more than cooking the food that you yourself can produce. It's no accident that in the plains of the northern Po Valley, where cattle can be pastured, much of the cookery uses cream and butter. Further south, where the topography is mountainous, butter is replaced with olive oil.

In the plains around Turin and Milan, the winters are long, cool and misty. The air is heavy with humidity and it's here that you'll

find the paddy fields that produce Italian rice. In this region of Italy, Lombardy, risotto is eaten more often than pasta. Once again, people eat what they themselves produce.

There is another facet to Italian gastronomy that's worth looking at, and it's the emphasis on the quality of raw ingredients. If you've ever watched an Italian woman buying fruit or vegetables at a market stall, you'll see this emphasis at work. She'll pick up and feel each item, she'll smell it, test its firmness, check its colour – anything that doesn't conform to her exacting standards will be replaced. Not for her a pre-packaged tray of six apples under a plastic wrapper – she'll want to select each and every apple herself.

There is an understanding that quality is something that needs to be sought after, and part of this is the understanding that quality will cost more than the run of the mill. In the Comino Valley, the part of Italy that I call home, there are people who keep pigs outdoors and let them forage in forests for acorns. These pigs, called *ruspante*, command a premium over battery farmed pigs. The reason they cost more is that free-range pigs are costlier to produce, but there's no doubt that their meat tastes better and it's free from the antibiotics and hormone treatments that battery pigs get.

This brings us to a word that you'll hear a lot in Italy – *genuino*. You've probably guessed that it means genuine, but when it's applied to food, it has a rather more complex meaning. It's the word that's used to describe food that's produced traditionally, food that's unadulterated, food that is exactly as our forbears would have understood it. It has the kind of cachet that the word 'organic' used to have here. It evokes a simpler world, a world without the technology to adulterate food.

In the modern world, where every week a new fad diet is unveiled, where food allergies are becoming the norm rather than the exception, the simple, genuine cooking of regional Italy is increasingly recognised as a healthy diet. Good food is the crown of civilisation, and cookery is what separates us from brute creation. The joys of the table are there to be celebrated, so gather your friends around you and break bread together, acknowledging the gift of life, laughter and love.

The Italian Larder

You may not have a large room devoted entirely to foodstuffs, but even if all you have is a small press in your kitchen, you can put together some basic foods that will form your larder. All these essentials can be kept without refrigeration.

- Olive oil
- Vinegar – wine vinegar and balsamic
- Packets of dried pasta in various shapes
- Rice – plain long-grained rice and maybe a packet of Arborio or Carnaroli rice
- Potatoes
- Passata
- Dried herbs – parsley, sage, rosemary, thyme, basil and oregano
- Chillies, either whole or powdered
- Black peppercorns

- Dried mushrooms
- Garlic and onions in strings
- Tins of tuna
- Tins of chopped tomatoes
- Stock cubes – meat, chicken and vegetable
- Anchovies
- Olives (stoned)
- Breadcrumbs*
- Capers
- Mustard

- Parmesan – *not* the little pots of pre-grated cheese, but the cheese itself
- Jars of roasted aubergines and courgettes packed in oil
- Prosciutto and sausages – the dried variety, either hanging up for early consumption, or packed in jars and covered in olive oil to preserve them for later
- Eggs, flour and cheeses – the hard kind that will keep – these complete the basic larder

When you look at this list, you can see at once that there are many dishes that can be made even with these few ingredients. And that's the point – even with unexpected guests, you can cook a meal. If you have these ingredients in your store cupboard, then you can make nearly all the recipes in this book. You'll just need to buy your chosen meat, fish and vegetables.

Breadcrumbs are used in a lot of recipes, so make them yourself. If you have slices of bread left over, put them somewhere warm and let them dry out completely. I put them on a rack above the range. When they're hard and dry, break them up and put them in a food processor. If you have a jar with a screw top lid they'll keep very well until you need them.

The Basic Utensils

If you want to cook Italian food well, there are a few kitchen utensils that you will need. The first is a large pot with a lid that holds at least 5 litres of water. If you want to cook pasta for more than four people, you'll need a larger pot than that. You can find pasta pots that come with a colander insert, which is very handy, but if you already have a big pot, you'll need a big colander. Trying to drain boiling hot pasta into a small colander doesn't work and you run the risk of getting steam burns.

If you've got a big pasta pot, you'll need a long wooden spoon to stir the pasta with without getting your hand close to the boiling water. Another useful implement is a spaghetti server, which is like a large spoon with tines around the edge.

A large, heavy frying pan is a must. Ideally it should have a heavy bottom, as that ensures that the heat will be evenly spread across the surface. I use a 30 centimetre-diameter pan, which gives me enough space to cook six steaks at a time.

Other than these, the usual kitchen utensils are all you'll need.

Measurements

All the recipes in this book are designed for four people, unless otherwise stated. Pasta dishes assume a standard 500-gram packet, and throughout I've taken 1 ounce to be 30 grams. Wherever I have not been specific about amounts, it's because exact amounts are not important, for example when a little more or a little less olive oil will not affect the dish.

CONVERSION CHARTS

Weight

30 g	1 oz	225 g	8 oz	425 g	15 oz	1.1 kg	2 ½ lb
60 g	2 oz	250 g	9 oz	450 g	1 lb	1.4 kg	3 lb
90 g	3 oz	280 g	10 oz	500 g	18 oz	1.5 kg	3 lb 5 oz
110 g	4 oz	310 g	11 oz	570 g	1 ¼ lb	1.8 kg	4 lb
140 g	5 oz	340 g	12 oz	680 g	1 ½ lb	2 kg	4 ½ lb
170 g	6 oz	370 g	13 oz	900 g	2 lb	2.2 kg	5 lb
200 g	7 oz	400 g	14 oz	1 kg	2 ¼ lb	4.5 kg	10 lb

Volume

5 ml	1 teaspoon	150 ml	5 fl oz	325 ml	11 fl oz
10 ml	1 dessertspoon	175 ml	6 fl oz	350 ml	12 fl oz
15 ml	1 tablespoon	200 ml	7 fl oz	400 ml	14 fl oz
30 ml	1 fl oz	240 ml	8 fl oz	450 ml	15 fl oz
60 ml	2 fl oz	270 ml	9 fl oz	475 ml	16 fl oz
90 ml	3 fl oz	300 ml	10 fl oz	1 litre	34 fl oz
120 ml	4 fl oz				

Oven

Degrees Celsius	Degrees Fahrenheit	Gas Mark	Description
140	275	1	Very cool
150	300	2	Cool
160	325	3	Warm
180	350	4	Moderate
190	375	5	Fairly hot
200	400	6	Fairly hot
220	425	7	Hot
230	450	8	Very hot
240	475	9	Very hot

Sauces

When I was a teenager, I had a book called *Picture Chords for Guitar*. The book taught chord shapes, for example the chord shape for an F, and showed how this same shape could become a G or an A simply by moving the shape up the neck of the guitar. Once you had mastered a chord shape, you could use it over and over again to make new chords on different frets. The book never taught me to be a great guitarist, but the idea of a shape that could be used more than once was an attractive one.

If you can make a white sauce, then you can make a béchamel, a cheese sauce or any derivative of the same shape. If you can make mayonnaise, then you can make an aioli. Master the basic shape, and the others follow as easily as sliding your fingers up and down the neck of a guitar. Just as variations on a theme is standard procedure in music, it is also the secret to innovative cooking. I think of it as 101 Chord Shapes for the Kitchen, so I've arranged the following sauces into families. Learn the base sauce, and the others follow as easily as ABC.

White Sauce

Before we go on to the recipes, there is a base sauce that you will need to learn, and that's white sauce. It's pretty awful – it's the culinary equivalent of wallpaper paste, glutinous and devoid of flavour. But it does have one big plus despite its drawbacks: it's the base for a lot of sauces that are good to eat. It's worth knowing how to make a white sauce simply so that you can convert it easily into something nice. Classic white sauce is made with water, not milk, so milk is already an improvement on the original.

All the cookbooks I've ever seen tell you to start with a walnut-sized knob of butter and some flour. Any time I've done this, I've ended up with a lumpy sauce that needed to go through a sieve. Maybe this is why packet sauce is available – people have tried to make it, failed like I did and now buy it in a packet.

I don't know if it's original, but for a while now I've been making it my own way. It's easy and it works every time.

For a perfect white sauce with no lumps, cover the bottom of a small saucepan with olive oil. Add 2 heaped dessertspoons of flour and stir well with a wooden spoon until it's the colour and texture of runny fudge. Add 250 ml of cold milk and stir, then put it on a high heat. Start stirring at once, and keep stirring gently until the sauce boils and thickens in 5 minutes or so. Remove it from the heat, salt it and it's done – lump-free white sauce ready to become something else.

Now that you have the basic white sauce under your belt, you're ready to make its variations.

Besciamella – BÉCHAMEL

You can enrich the base white sauce if you like by replacing half the milk with cream. For a basic béchamel, just add freshly ground black pepper and freshly grated nutmeg.

Béchamel will turn up in quite a few recipes, so it's worth taking the time to learn how to do it. You can't make *pasta al forno* (p. 60) without it and you'll need it if you want to make a soufflé (p. 91).

Besciamella alla Senape –
MUSTARD BÉCHAMEL

Mix some mustard powder with water, or use Dijon mustard from a jar and add the mustard plus 30 grams of butter to the base white sauce. This is good with poultry and grilled meats.

Besciamella ai Funghi –
MUSHROOM BÉCHAMEL

Cook off some mushrooms in butter on a low heat for about 10 minutes in a covered pot, until they've released their liquid. Take off the lid and let the liquid boil away. Salt the mushrooms to taste and add them to the béchamel, along with a couple of tablespoons of cream. This goes very nicely with poached eggs.

Salsa Mornay – SAUCE MORNAY

Beat 1 egg yolk with 100 ml of cream. Grate 30 grams of Parmesan and 100 grams of Gruyère. Fold the egg and cream mixture along with the grated cheese into the béchamel. Check the seasoning of salt and freshly ground black pepper. This is a classic sauce for fish and is also very good on poached eggs.

Salsa di Formaggio – CHEESE SAUCE

Grate the cheese of your choice into the béchamel. Put it back on the heat, stirring all the while until it melts, and it's a cheese sauce for boiled vegetables, macaroni cheese or Welsh rarebit.

Salsa al Curry – Curry Sauce

There are more complex versions of this sauce, but if you take the base white sauce and add curry powder to taste, you'll get a passable curry sauce. This is often used in Italy on vegetables and poultry.

Salsa Velutata – Velouté Sauce

If you make your white sauce with stock – either meat, fish or vegetable – then you've made a velouté sauce, you can use for a lasagna.

Salsa Aurora – Sauce Aurore

Add a dash of cream and enough tomato purée to colour the velouté sauce pink and it becomes a Sauce Aurore you can use for a lasagna.

Maionese — MAYONNAISE

I know it's really easy to buy a good mayonnaise, but do try this at least once. You'll discover exactly what it ought to taste like and you'll also discover that it's a yellow sauce, not a white one. Homemade mayonnaise is a real treat and it's worth making for the dishes that you're proud of.

The secret to making mayonnaise is patience. Be prepared to take your time and it will work just fine. There's a legend that the sauce was first made by Napoleon's Irish chef, McMahon, who had nothing but eggs and olive oil and needed a sauce. With these two ingredients he created the sauce that he gave his name to.

Take an egg that's been stored at room temperature – not in a fridge – and put just the yolk into a small bowl. Try to ensure that as little of the white gets in as possible. Whisk the egg a little with a fork and add a pinch of salt. You'll need to add the olive oil in very small amounts to begin with, so put some oil into a pouring jug and pour just a drop or two onto the egg yolk. Whisk with the fork until it's all been assimilated and then add a few more drops. Keep whisking and keep adding more drops of oil. After a few minutes you'll notice that it's beginning to thicken up and gradually you can increase the amount of oil that you add. You should be able to add easily 250 ml of oil to make a good amount of mayonnaise.

What is happening here is that the egg yolk is emulsifying the oil as you whisk. Under ideal circumstances, 1 egg yolk can emulsify up to 50 litres of oil, so 250 ml should be no problem.

You might like your mayonnaise with a bit of a bite, so you can add lemon juice. Don't add it after you've made your mayonnaise or it will fall apart – add it to the egg yolk at the start, with the salt. Recently I've begun to enjoy wasabi mayonnaise – all you need to do is add a squirt of wasabi from a tube.

If you also add a little crushed garlic to your mayonnaise, you'll have made aioli, which is just garlic-flavoured mayonnaise.

If you replace the olive oil with melted butter and proceed exactly as above, you'll have made an Hollandaise sauce.

If you rush making the mayonnaise and add too much oil too quickly, the mayonnaise can crack, that is, fall apart into its components of egg and oil. If that happens, don't despair. Take another egg yolk and start again, using your cracked mayonnaise as if it were oil and introducing it to the egg yolk a little at a time.

Pesto

There can't be anyone left in Ireland now who hasn't heard of pesto. It's one of my favourite pasta sauces and it's named after the way it's made, that is, in a mortar and pestle. This is still the best way to make it; a liquidiser is faster, but the taste changes – I think because the speed of the chop heats the basil. The principle is simple: grind fresh basil with a mortar and pestle, adding olive oil as you go, then freshly grated Parmesan, a little salt, garlic and optionally pine nuts until your sauce is thick and rich. It keeps well in a fridge for a week or two, so you can make more than you need for one meal and put the rest into a jar for a quick snack another time. I don't really approve, but you can bulk out the sauce with parsley if basil is scarce.

This principle of making a sauce with a mortar and pestle is a good one, and there is no reason why basil should be the only herb so used. It is a theme as variable as any other. You can make an unusual pasta sauce this

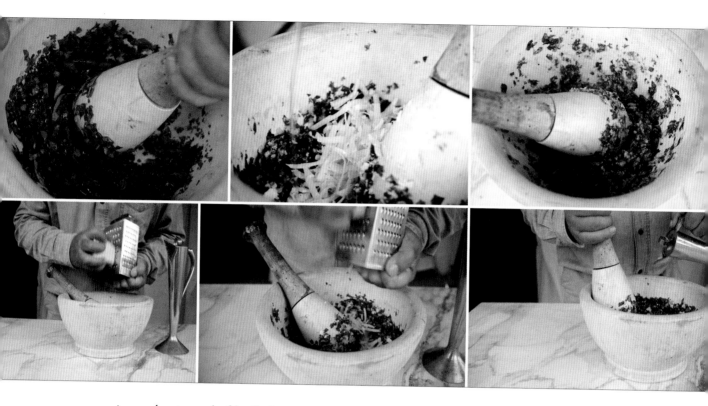

way using rocket instead of basil. As ever, use good olive oil, freshly grated Parmesan rather than pre-packaged and less garlic than you would for pesto. It's not the purist way, but in the spirit of adventure you could try thyme, rosemary or oregano – I haven't yet, but I intend to experiment.

Tapenade

This is a dish that's associated with the south of France, but since much of Provence used to be Italy, I feel no shame in including it. Essentially, tapenade is a purée of olives, either green or black, but more commonly black.

The easiest way to make it is in a blender. Put a tin of stoned olives – the stones do blenders no good – in a blender along with some olive oil. If you've used tasty olives, this purée will already taste pretty good, but you can experiment by adding other flavours. Capers are commonly added, as are anchovy fillets and garlic. Mustard, tuna, lemon juice and thyme are also occasionally used. Make this a few times and you'll find the particular mix of ingredients that works best for you. Tapenade often forms part of an *antipasto* plate.

Antipasti

All formal Italian meals begin with the *antipasto*, which translates as 'before the meal'. It's a little like the eastern Mediterranean *mezze* – it's an assortment of little goodies that are laid out on the table to prick the appetite. As the Italians are fond of quoting, 'eating will bring on the appetite'.

At its simplest, the *antipasto* might be no more than a few slices of prosciutto and salami, some olives and some sliced cheeses. At its most elaborate, it can leave you with barely any appetite left. All the following recipes are for four servings.

Bread

No Italian table is ever set without bread. It's a staple and it's always present. It doesn't get taken away when you finish the starters either – it remains on the table until the main course is over, and sometimes right till the end of the meal. The reason is simple – if there's a delicious sauce on your plate, you might want to finish it off with a crust of bread, what Italians call *fare la scarpetta*.

Antipasti are often served with *grissini*, or breadsticks. They're the best for dipping into sauces.

Bruschetta

This is one of the commonest parts of any *antipasto*. It's always made whenever there's a barbecue. You toast the slices of bread on the dying embers, having rubbed both sides of each slice with olive oil and garlic. If you're not having a barbecue, just put the bread in a toaster or under a grill. Once toasted, the bread slices are covered in chopped tomatoes, a pinch of salt and some chopped basil.

Crostini

Crostini are a staple of *antipasti*. You can use just about any kind of bread: focaccia, baguette, sourdough bread, soda bread, maize bread or even rye and buckwheat breads. What you make is essentially small pieces of toast topped with tasty titbits.

Livers, either chicken or game, are common toppings, as indeed are chopped cooked meats. They can be as simple or as complex as you like. Here a few really simple *crostini* for you to try.

Crostini con Puré di Olive –
CROSTINI WITH TAPENADE

Make the tapenade as described on p. 20 and spread a little on each *crostino*. Make the *crostini* quite small, say 5 centimetres square, so that one isn't particularly filling. A slice of baguette is about the right size.

Crostini di Tonno – CROSTINI WITH TUNA

Take a tin of tuna, preferably packed in brine, and flake it with a fork into a bowl. Add enough mayonnaise to make a creamy mix. Use it to top your *crostini*.

Crostini alla Svelta – QUICK CROSTINI

Mix chopped tomatoes, chopped basil leaves, garlic, a little salt and a dash of olive oil. Top each *crostino* with this mixture and lay a slice of mozzarella on top. Put the *crostini* under the grill until the mozzarella melts, then serve.

Crostini Oristano – ORISTANO CROSTINI

Make Paolo's tomato sauce as described on p. 38 and spoon it onto each *crostino*. Cut 4 slices of prosciutto into thin strips and chop up 4 large black olives. Top each *crostino* with the prosciutto strips and olives, then serve.

Panini Ripieni – STUFFED ROLLS

Preheat the oven to 200°C. Hollow out 4 rolls by cutting off the tops and removing the soft interior crumb. Heat 3 tablespoons of cream in a pot with 100 grams of mild Provolone cheese and 30 grams of chopped pancetta until it's all become incorporated. Spoon this mixture into the hollow rolls, replace the tops and put them in the oven for a few minutes before serving. If you can't get Provolone cheese, try Gruyère or Gouda. In fact just about any cheese will make a tasty snack done this way.

Caponata in Agrodolce – Sweet and Sour *Caponata*

This is a classic from Sicily, but it's popular all over Italy.

1 kilo aubergines, diced

150 ml olive oil

1 onion, finely sliced

1 stick of celery, chopped or grated

400 grams ripe tomatoes, peeled
   and sliced

salt and freshly ground black pepper

100 ml white wine vinegar

100 grams stoned olives

30 grams capers

1 tablespoon sultanas, soaked in
   water and then drained

2 teaspoons sugar

basil leaves

Put the diced aubergines in a colander and salt them, then let them stand for half an hour. The salt will draw out liquid and the aubergines will become sweeter. Rinse them and dry them, then fry them in the olive oil over a medium heat until browned. Now either remove them from the pan and set them aside, or take a new pan and cook off the onion, celery and tomatoes in olive oil until the tomatoes have reduced and the mixture thickens. Season, then add the vinegar, olives, capers, sultanas and sugar and bring it to the boil. Reduce the heat to a simmer and add the cooked aubergines, stirring well. Let the mixture simmer for about 10 minutes before serving. Finish the dish with basil leaves.

Peperoni – Sweet Peppers

You'll notice that *peperoni* in Italy are sweet peppers, they're not spicy salami. The name literally means 'big peppers', as opposed to *peperoncini*, the small chilli peppers. It's a generally acknowledged truth in Italy that peppers can be eaten raw only by the young. Anyone over 21 will find raw peppers indigestible. You will never find raw peppers in a salad or on top of a pizza in Italy – peppers are always cooked. Whenever there's a barbecue in Italy, the peppers are tossed directly onto the embers. When you see how much heat is needed to char the tough skin, you realise why they're so hard to digest.

The most common way to cook them is under a hot grill. Let each quarter blacken before turning them, until the entire outside is charred. Now put the peppers into a paper or plastic bag, tie it up and leave it for half an hour. The peppers will continue to steam inside the bag and the blackened skin will become easier to remove.

Run them under a tap while rubbing them, and the blackened skin will come off and you'll find the perfectly cooked pepper underneath.

Once you've removed the skin, pull off the stem, cut them in half and remove the membranes and all the seeds.

Peperoni con Aglio – Peppers with Garlic

The simplest way to present peppers cooked as above is to slice them into thin strips and put them in a dish with olive oil and crushed garlic. If you then put this in the fridge for a day, the flavours will blend together beautifully.

Peperoni Arrotolati – Rolled Peppers

Cut 4 cooked peppers into 3 or 4 pieces each. Take 2 standard tins of tuna, a tomato, some stoned olives and a little chilli powder and blend it together with some lemon juice, basil leaves and olive oil. Put this mixture on each slice of pepper and roll it up into a tube. Lay the tubes in a serving dish and keep it in the fridge until it's time to serve them. Alternatively, cut the tubes into rounds before serving.

Peperonata

This can be served either hot or cold. Skin 4 cooked peppers and cut them into strips. Cook 2 sliced onions in a little olive oil over a medium heat until they're soft, then add the peppers. Cover the pan and reduce the heat. After about 10 minutes, add enough tomato sauce or passata to coat the peppers and season to taste. Uncover, and let it cook for another 5 minutes.

Zucchini Ripieni – STUFFED COURGETTES

Preheat the oven to 180°C. Slice 4 courgettes in half lengthwise. Scoop out the flesh without breaking the skins. Mix the flesh in a bowl with 2 eggs, 1 tin of tuna, 1 tablespoon of breadcrumbs, 1 tablespoon of freshly grated Parmesan and 1 tablespoon of white wine. Add a little olive oil and mix well. Spoon this mixture back into the courgette shells. Mix 1 tablespoon of breadcrumbs and 1 tablespoon of freshly grated Parmesan and sprinkle this on top of the shells before baking for half an hour.

Olive Ripiene – STUFFED OLIVES

Okay, stuffing an olive is tedious and time consuming, but the result is worth the work. Use big olives, they're easier to stuff than small ones.

Mix together 60 grams of finely minced ham and 60 grams of freshly grated Parmesan. Beat 1 egg and have some flour and breadcrumbs ready on separate plates. Stuff each olive with the ham and cheese mixture. Roll it in flour, then in the beaten egg and lastly in breadcrumbs. Fry them in hot olive oil and drain on kitchen paper before serving.

Fiori di Zucchini – Courgette Flowers

Courgette plants flower for a month or so. They're big, fleshy, yellow flowers and they're delicious. You can buy them in many farmers' markets when they're in season, or you could try growing your own courgettes, they're really not difficult to grow.

I make an unscientific batter, by which I mean I beat 1 egg, a cupful of milk and a pinch of salt with an electric whisk. Then, holding the whisk in one hand and a bag of plain flour in the other, I gently tip in flour while whisking until I get a batter about the consistency of cream. I call it unscientific because I have no idea of the measurements – I just keep tipping in flour until the mix looks right.

If you don't have a deep fat fryer, just half fill a small pot with cooking oil – soya, corn, safflower or sunflower – and let it heat up. You can test the heat by dropping little dribbles of batter into it. If they immediately sizzle as soon as they hit the oil, it's hot enough. Dip the flowers in the batter and drop them into the oil. After a couple of minutes, turn them with a slotted spoon until they're golden brown all over. Drain them on kitchen paper and serve them quickly.

Sometimes in Italy you'll get them filled with an anchovy stuffing, but it's really unnecessary. They're delicious just as they are, so don't try to gild the lily.

Fritelle di Assisi — ASSISI FRITTERS

These are a great way to use a glut of courgettes when you're fed up eating them in other ways.

Grate 250 grams of courgettes into a colander and leave them to drain for half an hour. Beat 1 egg yolk in a bowl with 100 grams of plain flour, 150 ml of water, 2 teaspoons of olive oil and some salt and freshly ground black pepper to make a batter. Whisk the egg white until stiff and fold it into the batter.

Now add the grated courgettes to the batter, along with 100 grams of freshly grated Parmesan. Drop spoonfuls of the mixture into hot frying oil and let them cook for about 5 minutes, until golden. Drain them on kitchen paper and serve.

Bagna Càuda — HOT SAUCE

Bagna càuda is a dip that's traditional in the Piedmont region of Italy. You can dip breadsticks or vegetables cut into strips into it. Essentially you combine two things, garlic and anchovies, in roughly equal proportions. A mortar and pestle does this job well, but you can do it in a blender.

For 1 tin of anchovy fillets I'd use 3 medium cloves of garlic. As you mix these two elements together, add some olive oil – about 4 tablespoons will leave you with a sauce of the right consistency. Season it with salt and freshly ground black pepper and the sauce is made. It can be eaten cold or warm.

Fritelle di Funghi e Fegato — MUSHROOM AND LIVER FRITTERS

Melt 30 grams of butter in a frying pan and cook 225 grams of chicken livers and 100 grams of chopped mushrooms with a little salt and freshly ground black pepper over a medium heat. Stir and cook until the livers are brown all over. Remove them from the pan and drain off any liquid. Mix them into 75 ml of white sauce (p. 15) and put the mixture in the fridge until it has set, which makes it easier to spoon the mixture.

Use a tablespoon to scoop out balls of the mixture and drop them into hot oil. Fry for about 5 minutes, until they're golden brown. Drain them on kitchen paper and serve.

The Farinaceous Dishes

For centuries pasta has been a staple of the Italian diet. In central and southern Italy the classic dish was *pasta e fagioli*, or pasta and beans – a nutritionally perfect combination of carbohydrates and pulses – but outside of Italy, pasta with a tomato sauce is better known. It's usually described on menus as *pasta alla Napoletana*, named after the city of Naples where tomatoes were first used as food rather than as table decoration 400 years ago.

To begin at the beginning, pasta comes in two types, fresh and dried. Dry pasta is the one in every shop; it keeps for ages, so it's a good idea to have the larder stocked with a variety of shapes. Italians are very fussy about what shapes go with what sauce, and there is sense in this. Every sauce has different properties when it comes to coating the pasta. For example, thick sauces do not work well on cut pasta such as penne or rigatoni, since the insides of the tubes don't get covered and you end up eating a high proportion of pasta to sauce. Thick sauces that contain little oil or butter work best on fusilli or spaghetti, where the surface area is large in proportion to the volume. These are not hard and fast rules, but they are worth observing.

Fresh pasta doesn't keep for long, so it's usually made for immediate consumption. It makes a change from dried pasta and is not hard to make – it's only flour and eggs. Any white wheat flour will do, but the best results come from using hard durum wheat flour, type 00. You can make more than you intend to eat right away. If you hang your tagliatelle over a line, it will dry quickly and keep for a week or more with no problems. Lasagne will need plenty of work surfaces where you can lay out the pieces on floured boards or trays until they're dry. After that, they can be packed loosely into boxes until they are needed.

On occasions, gnocchi, made from potato and flour, make a change from pasta. The secret to good, delicate gnocchi, as opposed to hard little bullets, is using as little flour as possible. The principle is straightforward: stiffen mashed potato with flour to make a firm dough from which the gnocchi are made. The less water the boiled potatoes contain, the less flour you need to make a stiff paste. Waxy potatoes work better than floury ones and steaming works better than boiling.

Another farinaceous dish eaten in Italy is polenta, or boiled maize meal. It's common all over Italy, but it's most often found in the north-east, where the inhabitants are referred to as *polentoni*, 'big polenta eaters'. In itself, it's not particularly tasty; like plain mashed potato, it needs something else to make it appealing.

In the north-west, in the plains of Lombardy, you'll find the paddy fields where Italian rice is grown. As a result, risotto is a common dish in this area.

Lastly, there's bread. The traditional Italian loaf is the 2-kilo *pagnotta* – literally 'big bread'. It's the staple bread of the bakeries and it can even be bought in supermarkets. You can buy a half loaf or even a quarter loaf, and this particular loaf has its price controlled by law. No such restriction exists for fancier breads, which can be expensive, but the basic loaf is cheap and in most bakeries it's good. It does have a hard crust, which Italians in general like, but visitors to Italy should beware – I've had several guests who have broken the crowns on their teeth by biting too hard and too quickly on a *pagnotta*.

How to Cook Pasta

Cooking pasta is easy, but it's just as easy to do it wrong. I've been in Ireland long enough to know what the usual faults are, and they're commonly these: not enough salt in the water and not enough water. So here are the basic rules to remember if you want perfect pasta.

1 For every 100 grams of pasta that you cook, you'll need 1 litre of water. So if you're cooking a standard 500-gram packet, you'll need a pot that will easily hold 5 litres of water. The reason you need a lot of water is because you want the starch in the pasta to come out. If there's insufficient water, your pasta will retain its starch and will be stodgy.

2 For every 1 litre of water you need 1 teaspoon of salt, so for a 500-gram packet you'll need 5 teaspoons of salt. Don't panic – you're not going to be ingesting all that salt. Almost all of it will go down the sink when you drain the pasta, but you'll need it to make the pasta taste as it should.

3 Any idea you may have about adding oil to stop the pasta from sticking should now be discarded. Oil and water don't mix, and oil on the surface of the water will not stop pasta from sticking below the surface. What you must do is stir – immediately after the pasta goes into the boiling water, then after 4 minutes and then again 4 minutes later, or more often if you can.

4 Never serve plain pasta in a plate with the sauce plonked on the top. You can't expect anyone to stir the sauce through their pasta properly on a plate. Once the pasta is cooked and strained, put it back in the cooking pot and stir in your sauce thoroughly before you plate up. If you like, you can always add an extra dollop of sauce to the plate before serving.

5 Don't slavishly adhere to the cooking time on the packet. These are only guides and I've encountered some that are totally wrong. Trust your own palate. Pasta is cooked when it's *al dente*, which means when it still has a little firmness. If you break the pasta, you shouldn't see a white ring inside; if you do, it's not cooked yet. Undercooked pasta is as big a sin as overcooked.

6 One last general rule of cooking pasta – never worry about making too much. It's a curious thing, but leftover pasta often tastes better the next day, as the flavours have had a chance to combine thoroughly. Italians often reheat leftover pasta in a frying pan with a little oil, stirring constantly to avoid sticking, or it can be put into an oven dish and layered with more tomato sauce alternating with a béchamel sauce. This is called *pasta al forno*, and once tasted, you'll never worry about having pasta left over.

Pasta Sauces

Throughout this book I've arranged the recipes in families, that is, I've started with the base sauce and then gone on to show you the derivatives of that sauce. So if you master the first one, the following ones will be easy.

Quick Pasta Sauces

Pasta in Bianco – Pasta with Butter

When I was a small boy I'd spend a few weeks every summer with my grandparents. My grandmother was, I realise now, not really interested in the finer points of gastronomy, but most days she'd make me the lunch I really liked – pasta with butter. My own children loved it too, and for a busy parent there's really nothing easier. Once the pasta is cooked and drained, add a knob of butter and stir it in. You can be a real gastronome and sprinkle a little freshly grated Parmesan on top to finish it off.

Pasta Aglio ed Olio – Pasta with Oil and Garlic

Where butter is not part of the daily gastronomy, olive oil takes its place, and this dish, common in Lazio, is a grown-up's version of pasta with butter. It's known in Italy as the cuckold's pasta, since any man returning home at lunchtime being presented with this would ask himself, 'What has she been doing all morning? This took five minutes to prepare.' Obviously she's spent the time with a lover and hadn't left enough time to make a labour-intensive lunch of the sort many Italian men would expect.

Essentially this is no more than pasta with flavoured oil stirred through it, but despite being very easy to make, there are things to watch out for. Start off with a small pan and cover the bottom of it with olive oil over a medium-low heat. Add some finely sliced garlic and stir. It's important not to cook this over a high heat, since burnt garlic is profoundly indigestible, so watch for any sign of browning. Pour the flavoured oil onto the cooked pasta through a sieve to catch the garlic pieces.

Pasta Aglio, Olio e Peperoncino – PASTA WITH OIL, GARLIC AND CHILLI

In the hinterland of Rome, *pasta aglio ed olio* is often made with a third ingredient, chilli. If you decide to try this variation, chop up a small chilli and add it to the oil with the garlic in the recipe above. Like before, sieve this before pouring it onto the pasta and stirring well.

Tomato Sauces

I've long believed that to prepare any dish well, you should know when you begin what the final result should taste like. Forgive me if that sounds obvious, but it's been my experience that not every cook follows this simple maxim. What this means in practice is that following an untried recipe is a hit and miss affair. Recipes can be only guides at best; unless you have a clear idea of where you're going, you can end up with a dish a long way from what you intended.

What prompts this musing is that recently I've noticed supermarket shelves increasingly stocked with pre-prepared tomato sauces. The choice is daunting, not only with the myriad of brand names, but also with the range of flavours on offer – traditional pasta sauce, with added garlic, with spices and herbs, with mushrooms – every conceivable combination known to marketing man. Faced with such a choice, where do you begin?

If you make a tomato sauce just once from scratch, then you'll know what it ought to taste like. Once you know that, you're in a better position to choose from the array of convenience sauces on the shelves since you'll have a baseline from which to rate them.

When I was a small boy visiting my relations in Italy, I used to go exploring the narrow, cobbled lanes of Gallinaro. From early morning until lunchtime, pots of *sugo* – tomato sauce – sat simmering on ranges and hobs, slowly boiling down, intensifying the flavours. Some might have a ham bone, others sausages added for taste. These days, it's hard to find a sauce made like this; modern Italians go for a quick, light tomato sauce that puts less strain on the digestion.

Salsa Napoletana – Neapolitan Sauce

Once you're comfortable with this sauce, you can use it as a base for more complex sauces, but crucially, you'll know what a tomato sauce ought to taste like.

To make a simple *salsa Napoletana*, begin with good-quality tinned plum tomatoes – they should be firm, sweet, deep red and full-fleshed. There are some shippers who put unripe, orange-tinged tomatoes in cans with lots of water. They should be avoided. Drain the tomatoes and slice them open to remove the seeds. The only excuse for having seeds in a tomato sauce is laziness; they shouldn't be there, as they add acidity. Next you should push the tomatoes through a coarse sieve with a wooden spoon, although chopping them finely will do at a pinch.

Cover the bottom of a saucepan with olive oil. Add some finely chopped onion and garlic and let it fry gently over a medium heat until cooked. Add the sieved or chopped tomatoes, some basil, a bay leaf and a little salt and freshly ground black pepper. Cook for 15 minutes, and it's done. If you time it right, you can make this sauce while the water boils and the pasta cooks. The longer you cook it, the more it reduces and you'll need to add more olive oil to thin it down.

In Naples, the tomato sauce that goes on pizzas is made exactly like this Neapolitan sauce, except that instead of basil, the herb is oregano. When you use oregano instead of basil, the sauce is called *pizzaiola*.

Paolo's Tomato Sauce

Now that you know the classic recipe, let me tell you how I make a tomato sauce. Any cookbook will give you something very similar to the classic recipe above, but my way breaks all the rules. No seeds and no skin are important, so you can buy passata, which is nothing more than sieved tomatoes. It's readily available in supermarkets and there's a wide variety to choose from. What you need to find are versions that aren't watery.

We'll be using this sauce a lot in the following recipes, and not just for pasta. Tomato sauce turns up in many recipes, so it's a good idea to have some to hand. Whenever I make it, I always make more than I need. I put the remainder in a covered jar in the fridge, where it will keep well for a few days. Then, if I want a quick snack, the sauce only needs to be heated up. If you want to store it for more than a few days, cover the top of the sauce with olive oil. This keeps it away from the air and stops any moulds that might try to form on the surface.

Tip the passata into a wide-bottomed pan or skillet. Half a litre of passata will make enough sauce for a standard 500-gram packet of pasta. Put it on a high heat and add a splashguard if you don't want your work surfaces covered in spots of tomato. Let the passata reduce to half of what it was, then turn down the heat and start to add your olive oil.

At first the oil will just sit on top of the thickened passata, but keep stirring and the sauce will start to absorb the oil. Now you can add some crushed garlic, a few leaves of basil, salt and freshly ground black pepper, and your sauce is finished. You'll notice that doing it this way, your sauce will have a different consistency – it will be thicker, denser in flavour, richer and just possibly less digestible, but it will be delicious. Adding the oil last has a major benefit – cooked oil loses that fresh spicy flavour, but this way it's simply warmed up with the sauce and that fresh olive oil taste will still be present.

You'll also notice that I always add garlic at the end of the cooking process – that's because garlic slowly loses its taste the longer it cooks, so adding it at the end ensures it still has a bite.

Arrabbiata

Once you've mastered the basic tomato sauce, you're ready for all its variations. The easiest of all is *arrabbiata*, which you'll find on many restaurant menus. The word means 'angry' in Italian and it's used to describe this sauce because what you add is chilli, making it fiery and hot. If you worry about dosing anything with chillies, I'd suggest you use chilli oil, which I've described how to make on p. 178.

Amatriciana

In the Alban hills outside Rome there's the little village of Amatrice, which has given its name to this sauce. Again you'll make a tomato sauce, but this time you'll need about 150 grams of pancetta, or if you're a purist, *guanciale*. Put a little oil in a pan and add the pancetta or *guanciale* diced quite small and cook it until the fat starts to run. Now add 1 diced onion, then add the passata and proceed as you would for Paolo's tomato sauce above, but for *Amatriciana* you don't add garlic.

Putanesca

This translates as pasta hooker style and is a popular dish in central Italy. I urge you to make this using passata, as for Paolo's tomato sauce (p. 38). This time, chop half a tin of stoned black olives into quarters. Add the chopped olives, half a small jar of drained capers and a tin of anchovies to the passata and boil it down until it has reduced by half. Finish the sauce by adding olive oil, crushed garlic, salt and freshly ground black pepper as you would for Paolo's tomato sauce.

Pasta al Tonno – Pasta with Tuna

Make Paolo's tomato sauce as described on p. 38. Drain a 120-gram tin of tuna and flake the tuna into the sauce using a fork. One finely chopped anchovy fillet improves the sauce. I tend to use tuna in brine rather than in oil because the quality of the oil in tinned tuna is rarely very good.

Ragù alla Bolognese

If you drive from Milan to Rome on the Autostrada del Sole, you begin the journey by travelling across the vast, flat plains of the Po Valley. As you approach Bologna, the foothills of the Apennines come into view, which here run almost across Italy left to right, forming a natural barrier. This barrier of mountains is also a gastronomic demarcation line. In the plains, cookery is heavily tilted toward cream and butter, while over the mountains to the south, olive oil is predominant. Not for nothing is Bologna known as Bologna the Fat.

Ten miles past Bologna, just before the motorway begins its spectacular path across the Apennines to Florence, there is an exit to the little town of Sasso Marconi. Nestling up against the hills, Sasso is the southernmost outpost of the great cookery tradition of the Emilia-Romagna. Even regionally chauvinistic Italians will grudgingly admit that the food of the Emilia-Romagna region is second to none, and all around the world, Bologna is known for the sauce to which it gave its name – Bolognese.

I have eaten spaghetti Bolognese in many countries, but nowhere has it ever tasted as good as in the tiny trattoria in Sasso Marconi where I often make the lunchtime stop. The problem is that this sauce is often understood to be a tomato sauce with a bit of mince in it. It isn't. It's a meat sauce that has a little tomato in it. Until tomatoes arrived in quantity in Italy some 400 years ago, the sauce was made without them. It isn't a quick sauce – the longer it cooks, the better it tastes – but it really is worth the effort.

Cover the bottom of a large frying pan with good olive oil. Over a medium heat, add finely chopped onion, garlic, finely chopped or grated carrot and celery and stir. When the onion is cooked, add minced beef and minced pork, and for extra flavour, some optional chicken livers. A handful of chicken livers adds a richness to the sauce, and once they're cooked they'll blend into the sauce completely. Optional too is about 100 grams of finely cubed streaky bacon or pancetta. Pour in a cup of stock and a glass of red wine. Let it cook very slowly, adding stock or wine if it starts to reduce too quickly. A lid on the frying pan will help keep it moist. This is, you'll notice, a brown sauce, not a red one.

How long you choose to cook this is up to you – 4 to 6 hours is good, but don't let it dry up and keep the heat low. About 1 hour before you intend serving it, add some deseeded, chopped plum tomatoes or a little passata and let them cook and blend into the sauce. Season with salt and freshly ground black pepper. It should still be more brown than red.

Traditionally this sauce goes with spaghetti or fettuccine, but it works well with short, cut pasta like penne if you find spaghetti hard to handle.

Cream Sauces

Tortellini alla Panna –
TORTELLINI WITH CREAM

This is the simplest of all the cream sauces and is a speciality from the Emilia-Romagna area of Italy, which is centred on Bologna. You can use tortellini with a meat stuffing or with a ricotta and spinach filling.

First bring a pot of salted water to the boil. Melt 40 grams of butter in a small saucepan. For 250 grams of tortellini, add 250 ml of cream to the melted butter and let it boil to reduce it. Reducing cream has the effect of thickening it and changing its colour from white to a golden straw colour.

While this is happening, keep an eye on your pasta water. When it's boiling vigorously, add the tortellini and stir to prevent them from sticking. Between 5 and 8 minutes is usually enough for tortellini, but check the packet, which should give a recommended cooking time.

When the cream has assumed the colour and consistency that you want, turn the heat down very low and grate some Parmesan into it – about 60 grams should be readily absorbed by the cream. Stir until the Parmesan is incorporated.

Drain the tortellini when cooked, return them to the pot and pour on the sauce. Stir and serve with a sprinkle of freshly grated Parmesan on top.

Pasta al Carciofo –
PASTA WITH ARTICHOKES

I first ate this dish in one of great restaurants of Lazio, Ristorante Mantova, nearly 40 years ago. Although I knew the owners well, it took a lot of wheedling to extract the recipe from them. Unfortunately it does involve a little work, but the effort is well repaid in a sensational, subtly flavoured dish.

The trick in this recipe is to use the boiling water twice – once for cooking the artichokes and then again for the pasta. This ensures that whatever flavour and colour the artichokes have lost to the boiling water will be imparted to the pasta that you cook in it.

First bring a pot of salted water to the boil. Add 4 large globe artichokes, with any dead or discoloured outer leaves removed. Ten minutes will cook them sufficiently. Remove them from the water and leave the water simmering.

Now comes the hard work. Remove the leaves one by one from the artichokes, and using a grater, remove the small bit of soft flesh from the base of each leaf. The amount of flesh will increase gradually as you approach the heart. Grate the heart as well. When you've finished with all 4 globes you'll have a small pile of artichoke purée. A word of warning – Irish-grown artichokes have a wonderful appearance, but I have yet to find one that doesn't have a bunch of fibres instead of a heart; avoid them. If all this sounds like just too much work, you can use bottled artichoke hearts and blend them, but make sure you buy the ones in olive oil that haven't been pickled. The taste of vinegar will completely overpower and ruin this delicate sauce.

Melt 60 grams of butter in a small saucepan. Add 120 ml of cream and let it reduce as described for *tortellini alla panna on* p. 41. At this point you can now let the pasta water boil vigorously and put the penne, or better still, rigatoni, on to cook.

While the pasta cooks – don't forget to stir it occasionally – add your artichoke purée to the cream and turn the heat down low. Stir it in well and salt to taste. You can let the sauce stand on a very low heat while the pasta finishes cooking.

Finish as usual by draining the pasta, returning it to the pot and pouring in the sauce. Stir it well, then serve. This dish is served without Parmesan.

Pasta ai Fungi –
PASTA WITH MUSHROOMS

If you've ever had pasta with mushrooms before, I'm prepared to bet that it wasn't great. The problem with turning any vegetable into a sauce is getting the right consistency. With tomatoes, you simply boil them down. With artichokes, you use cream. But with a mushroom sauce, we introduce another piece of the jigsaw, which I learnt from my good friend Antonio Breschi, the pianist and composer whose culinary skills are on a par with his musical ones.

Autumn is the time for parasols, which make the best version of this sauce, but cultivated flats (rather than buttons) with an addition of shiitake or oyster mushrooms for flavour makes a very acceptable substitute. Ceps are the finest of all mushrooms, but I've always felt it would be a shame to make them into a sauce, as there are so many other more exciting things you can do with them.

The first step is to chop the mushrooms very finely, or if you prefer, use a food processor to do the chopping. For 500 grams of pasta you'll need 700 grams of mushrooms.

Cover the bottom of a large frying pan with oil and let the oil heat up over a medium heat. Add the chopped mushrooms and stir quickly until all the mushrooms have had a coating of oil. Turn down the heat, add a glass of red or white wine and put a lid on the pan. Let the mushrooms sweat for half an hour, stirring occasionally to ensure they're not burning. If they start to look dry, add a little more wine. After half an hour they should be a uniformly slate grey, verging on black.

Before the half-hour is up, put the water for the pasta on to boil. If you can arrange it so that the water is boiling at the end of the mushrooms' half an hour of cooking time, so much the better. Put the pasta on – fusilli or twists work well with this – and remember to stir from time to time.

Back to the sauce – it's time to add the cream. Depending on how much wine you've used and the original water content of the mushrooms, the amount of cream will vary. Add enough cream to make the sauce liquid.

This time we won't reduce the cream. Instead, we're going to use Antonio's trick – a bland cheese. He uses *cacciotta*, but we're going to use a bland white cheddar. This will not affect the taste of the sauce in any way, but it will give it a wonderful consistency that will coat the pasta to perfection. You can use a lot of cheese – 100 to 200 grams – but don't forget to turn the heat down to its lowest setting, as cheese will burn at very low temperatures. Grate it onto the mushroom and cream mixture and stir until it's melted in. If it makes the sauce too thick, just add a little more cream.

Lastly, it's my experience that mushrooms soak up salt. Add what you believe to be a lot of salt and taste the sauce. My bet is that it will still taste under-salted.

As usual, drain the pasta, return it to the pot and add the sauce, stirring it in well. This, too, is served with no Parmesan.

Pasta Tulliano – SMOKED SALMON PASTA

This is a dish I first tasted in Rome many years ago, when smoked salmon had only recently become a common commodity in Italy. I tried to elicit the recipe from the chef, but what he eventually gave me turned out to be nothing like what I'd eaten. But I kept working on it, and after a year or so I had it. This is the recipe that I ended up with.

You can either slice whole smoked salmon, or if you can get it, use offcuts from a fishmonger, which is considerably cheaper. Either way, you'll need about 200 grams of smoked salmon, chopped as small as you can. It is possible to do it in a blender, but there is a risk that the smoked salmon will heat up and become a lump of plastic from which there is no return. Better be safe, use a knife.

Melt 100 grams of butter in a pan and add the chopped smoked salmon. Turn the heat down low and let it cook. It will lighten in colour as it cooks. Use the back of a fork to mash the salmon into a paste as it cooks. This is a tad tedious, but it's the best way to combine the butter and the salmon, so keep mashing. It will begin to thicken at this point, so now is the time to add cream to bring the sauce to the desired consistency – about 150 ml should be enough. It will be pale in colour at this stage, so add 1 teaspoon of tomato purée to bring back the colour. This won't change the taste of the sauce in any way, but it will give it a tinge of pink, which is what you'd expect a smoked salmon sauce to look like.

Let the cream boil down a little to thicken it up. The sauce is now ready and can be kept on a low heat until it's needed. If it thickens up too much, add a splash more cream. Just before serving, add a shot of cognac or brandy and stir it in. This really brings out the flavour of the salmon.

THE FARINACEOUS DISHES

Other Pasta Dishes

I saw a culinary map of Europe some years ago that had, amongst other things, the olive oil contour marked on it. North of this line, frying was traditionally done in butter, while south of it, olive oil did the job. It's obvious when you think about it — climate is a major determinant of our diet. Rice is a staple in countries where it grows, dairy produce in countries rich in pasture. Likewise, the connection between a people's diet and the exigencies of their everyday life has always fascinated me. Southern Italy has traditionally eaten the staple of pasta and pulse — *pasta e fagioli* — because it was cheap and nourishing. The peasant diet wasn't based so much on choice as on necessity. Pulses produce a lot of protein per acre.

All over Europe, different regions have different specialities, bound inextricably to their local produce. Parma hams and Parma cheese (Parmesan) are traditional in the area around Parma because it's close to the plains of the Po Valley and because its dry air allows the successful salt curing of the hams. None of this accidental. Food has its origins in the local agriculture and is therefore bound up with climate.

Spaghetti alla Carbonara

Sometimes dishes evolve from different circumstances. My favourite example of this is *pasta alla carbonara*. This is a dish that was made by the charcoal burners who gave it its name. Before gas was commonplace in Italian kitchens, charcoal was the cooking fuel and there was therefore a need for its production. Because Italy is so heavily populated and cultivated, forests are largely confined to the high mountains. The charcoal burners would take their mules in a caravan to the high places in the early spring and would spend the summer coppicing the hornbeam, birch and beech. All through the summer they made piles of faggots, which would then be covered with sods and fired so that the combustion would take place with no air and therefore no flame, carbonising the wood. In the autumn they returned to the valley, mules laden with charcoal for sale.

Life in the mountains was Spartan, and *pasta alla carbonara* evolved from this way of life. One pot, one fire, dried pasta and salt-cured sausage define the dish. In its pure mountain form, the pasta was boiled and drained, eggs and chopped sausage were tossed into the pot and the pasta was stirred. That's it. If you're an Italian charcoal burner, that may be fine, but in a modern kitchen, the dish can be refined a little and, I think, improved.

While a 500-gram packet of spaghetti is on the boil – or use a cut pasta like penne if you find spaghetti hard to handle – beat 4 egg yolks well with half an eggshell of water, some freshly ground black pepper and freshly grated Parmesan. If the Parmesan thickens it up, add a little more water. These days, purists insist on *guanciale*, which is air-cured pig's cheek, but if you can't find that, cube a little pancetta, or at a pinch, collar of bacon, and fry it lightly in olive oil over a medium heat. When the spaghetti is cooked, drain it and return it to the pot. Pour in the pancetta and oil from the pan, stir, then pour in the egg mixture. Stir once more. If you're quick doing this, the residual heat of the spaghetti will cook the egg and the dish is made.

In America, the UK and Ireland, this dish is unfailingly made with cream, which couldn't be more wrong. If you beat the egg yolks and Parmesan well, you'll find that it's creamy enough. The only mistakes you can make are to keep the pot of pasta on the heat while you add the egg mixture, and if you've used egg whites as well as the yolks, your *carbonara* will be far from creamy.

Tortellini con Burro alle Erbe – Tortellini with Herb Butter

This is the perfect dish to make if you've got fresh herbs on your window ledge or in the garden. Mix and match them – I enjoy this simple dish with rosemary and thyme, basil and oregano, or sometimes all four.

This works best with the tortellini that are filled with ricotta and spinach. Put the tortellini on to cook in boiling salted water. While they're cooking, melt 50 grams of butter in a small pot and add your herbs to it.

When the tortellini are cooked, strain them and return them to the pot, then stir in the melted butter and serve. Simple and very good.

Maccheroni Gratinati –
MACARONI CHEESE

Make half a litre of white sauce as per the recipe on p. 15. Beat 2 egg yolks into it and add 100 grams of freshly grated Parmesan, stirring well.

Meanwhile, preheat the oven to 240°C and grease an ovenproof dish. Cook 500 grams of pasta until it's *al dente*. You can use penne for this. Stir most of the cheese sauce into the cooked, drained pasta before transferring it to the dish. Cover the top with the remaining sauce and cook for about 20 minutes, until the top is golden brown.

Spaghetti alle Vongole –
SPAGHETTI WITH CLAMS

This is the classic Neapolitan dish. They're fussy in Naples about what clams they use – they prefer the clams that have two tubes coming out of them, rather than the clams with the single tube. These are known in Italian as *vongole verace*. The argument rages in Naples as to whether this dish is made with tomatoes or without them, so I'll give you both recipes.

Without Tomatoes

While your 500 grams of spaghetti cooks until it's *al dente*, slice 3 cloves of garlic and fry until golden in plenty of olive oil, about 1 tablespoon of oil per person, in a large frying pan over a medium heat, taking care not to let the garlic burn. Tip 750 grams of clams into the pan and cover it. Let them cook until they all open up, discarding any that don't open. Shell about half of them and return the flesh to the pan. Leave the other half in their shells and set aside.

Add half a glass of white wine, some salt and freshly ground black pepper. Let the wine boil off a little. Pour the sauce onto the cooked, drained spaghetti and serve with a little chopped parsley and the rest of the clams in their half shell for garnish.

With Tomatoes

To make a light tomato sauce, start by browning 3 chopped cloves of garlic in olive oil in a large frying pan over a medium heat, taking care not to let it burn. Add half a litre of passata, cooking it for only 7 to 8 minutes. Optionally, you can add a little white wine. Put 750 grams of clams into the pan and let them cook until they've all opened up, discarding any that don't open. Shell about half of them and return the flesh to the pot. Leave the other half in their shells and set aside.

Add half a glass of white wine and some salt and freshly ground black pepper. Let the wine boil off a little. Pour the sauce onto the cooked, drained spaghetti and serve with a little chopped parsley and the rest of the clams in their half shell for garnish.

Pasta e Fagioli – Pasta with Beans

This is perhaps the most iconic dish of central and southern Italy. It was for centuries the staple of the working man, and nutritionally it was very well balanced. The beans are usually borlotti beans, but you can use cannellini. Both are available in tins, already cooked, from delicatessens and good grocery stores.

Italians use *lardo* for this dish, which, just as you might suspect, is pork lard. It's integral to the dish, so if the idea of pork fat worries you, try a different recipe. You might be able to find *lardo* in Ireland, but if not, you can substitute it with streaky bacon. It won't taste the same, but it'll be close.

This sauce usually goes with short cut pasta like penne, but I find that shells, especially the big ones, work very well.

Start by making half a litre of stock, either vegetable or meat. Finely chop an onion, a carrot, a stick of celery and 70 grams of either *lardo* or streaky bacon. Fry the *lardo* in oil over a medium heat and add the chopped onion, carrot and celery. Cook until the onion is browned, then add 100 grams of chopped tomatoes. Add in 2 ladles of stock and let it cook until the stock has been absorbed.

In another frying pan, fry 100 grams of diced pancetta, though failing that, bacon lardons will do. Add a tin of either borlotti or cannellini beans to that. Add a ladle of stock to this as well. Let the beans absorb the flavour of the pancetta for a few minutes, then add this to the vegetables in the other pan and mix them together.

Cook your pasta in boiling salted water until it's *al dente*, drain it and put it back in the pot. Pour the sauce over it, stirring well. Some people like this dish to be almost soupy, so you can use more of the stock. If you want a creamy texture to the sauce, you can blend some of the beans and add them back into the sauce as a purée.

Spaghetti con Pesto Genovese –
SPAGHETTI WITH PESTO

It's not that long ago when the word 'pesto' was unknown in Ireland, now the stuff is drizzled on just about everything. It's always been the speciality of the Ligurian coast, in Italy's north-west. It's often referred to as Pesto Genovese because it's such a common dish in Genova. The basil that they grow in Liguria is the basil with the small spear-shaped leaves, not the kind with the big wide leaves, so if you're making pesto as per the recipe on p. 19, use the small-leaved variety.

Pesto goes very well with spaghetti, so cook 500 grams of spaghetti until it's *al dente* and add 30 grams of butter to the drained pasta, stirring it in well. Now add your pesto, but don't overdo it. It has a strong flavour and you don't need to use a lot to flavour the pasta.

Tagliatelle Panna, Piselli e Prosciutto –
TAGLIATELLE WITH PROSCIUTTO AND PEAS

Thinly slice 1 onion and cook it until soft in a pot with 30 grams of butter and 2 tablespoons of olive oil over a medium heat. Add 200 grams of peas and cook for 20 minutes over a low heat, stirring it from time to time. Bring a large pot of water to the boil and cook 500 grams of tagliatelle until it's *al dente*.

Add 100 ml of cream and cook it for another 10 minutes, until the cream has reduced a little, then add 2 slices of prosciutto that you've cut up into small pieces. Drain the tagliatelle, return it to the pot and pour in the creamy mixture, along with some freshly grated Parmesan. Stir well and serve with some extra Parmesan sprinkled on top.

Penne alla Rughetta –
PENNE WITH ROCKET

Considering how popular rocket has become in the past decade, it's surprising that no restaurant has put this classic on the menu.

Heat a good splash of olive oil in a pan and gently fry 4 chopped cloves of garlic and 1 chopped chilli pepper over a medium-low heat. It's important not to cook this over a high heat, since burnt garlic is profoundly indigestible, so watch for any sign of browning.

Meanwhile, cook 500 grams of penne in boiling salted water, remembering to stir it from time to time. About 5 minutes before the pasta is cooked, throw 100 grams of chopped rocket leaves into the water.

When the pasta is cooked, strain it and return it to the pot. Pour the flavoured oil onto the cooked pasta through a sieve to catch the garlic and chilli pieces, stir well and serve with a sprig of parsley for garnish.

Filled Pasta

Up to now we've looked at pasta dishes in which the pasta gets a sauce stirred into it before it's served. Now we'll look at some of the fancier pasta dishes that involve filling the pasta first. You can, of course, buy ready-made ravioli and tortellini, but if you make your own pasta as described on pp. 62–3, then you can make these dishes from scratch.

Cannelloni – Big Tubes

Just as their name suggests, these are big tubes of pasta. You can buy them ready made, or you can make them by filling a rectangle of pasta and rolling it around itself.

Ravioli

Ravioli are made by rolling your pasta out into a large sheet and filling one half of the sheet in a grid formation with the filling. Then you fold the other half over that and cut between the fillings so that you have small pillows of pasta with the filling inside. Press the edges well to ensure that they don't burst open when you cook them.

You can buy trays for making ravioli which have hollows for the fillings and raised edges between them so when you place your second sheet on top of the sheet that contains the filling, you simply run your rolling pin across the top and the raised edges do the cutting, leaving you with perfect, evenly sized ravioli.

Tortellini and Tortelloni

Tortellini are the tiny ones, tortelloni are the big ones, but they're made the same way. For these, you cut your rolled-out pasta with a circular pastry cutter – the bigger the circle, the bigger the tortelloni. Again, place your filling on each round, fold it in half to create a half-moon shape, close the edges well and pull the pointed ends together, making a doughnut shape.

Making tortellini is very tedious. The amounts of filling are tiny, the rounds of pasta are small, they're hard to close well and getting them into the doughnut shape is exasperating. I'd guess that's why tortellini are nearly always factory made. Tortelloni, on the other hand, are much easier – even my clumsy fingers can manage them.

Lasagna

Lasagna is a layered pasta dish, where layers of pasta alternate with layers of filling. If you're making your own lasagne from a sheet of thinly rolled pasta, cut them about 10 centimetres square. There's no hard and fast rule to this – if they come out 10 centimetres by 5 centimetres, so be it.

I've seen many recipes that say you can tray up your lasagna with all the sauces and fillings without cooking it first. It's true that if your sauces contain enough water the pasta will cook in the oven dish, but I beg you, please, never to do this. What happens is that the starch that's present in the pasta that normally comes out into the cooking water remains in the pasta. You end up with a stodgy lasagna, the kind that retains a vertical face when you slice it. If you slice a properly made lasagna, it will slowly flop down, because there won't be any stodgy starch stiffening your lasagne.

So take a wide dish, it doesn't need to be deep, and boil some salted water in it. Cook the rectangles of pasta a few at a time for 5 to 6 minutes. As they cook, lay them on a damp tea towel to drain. Use these cooked pieces to tray up your lasagna and you'll get a result you'll be proud of.

The Fillings

These fillings can be used with lasagne, ravioli or tortellini. The base sauces, béchamel and tomato, are always used, and sometimes even in conjunction.

To get you started, here's an easy recipe designed for cannelloni, but you can use this filling for other pasta shapes.

Cannelloni alla Besciamella — Cannelloni with Béchamel

300 grams spinach

200 grams meat – leftover chicken, beef or pork – chopped

1 slice of cooked ham, chopped

2 tablespoons freshly grated Parmesan, plus extra to sprinkle on top

1 egg, beaten

salt and freshly ground black pepper

250 grams fresh pasta, rolled thinly and cut into rectangles roughly 10 cm by 5 cm (see pp. 62–3)

1 pint béchamel (p. 15)

30 grams butter

Preheat the oven to 200°C and grease an ovenproof dish. Cook the spinach in a frying pan over a medium heat for 5 minutes in only the water that remains on it after washing, then push it through a coarse sieve, blend it or roughly chop it. Mix it well with your chopped meat, Parmesan and beaten egg and season to taste.

Cook the rectangles of pasta a few at a time in a pan of boiling salted water for 5 to 6 minutes. As they cook, lay them on a damp tea towel to drain.

Put a small dollop of the filling onto each rectangle with a little béchamel and carefully roll them up into a tube lengthways. Lay the tubes side by side in the greased ovenproof dish and pour the remaining béchamel sauce over them. Put a few dabs of butter around the top and sprinkle on more Parmesan. Put in the oven for 20 minutes and it's done.

Ravioli con Prosciutto Cotto e Mozzarella — Ham and Mozzarella Ravioli

100 grams ricotta

100 grams cooked ham

100 grams freshly grated Parmesan, plus extra to serve

100 grams mozzarella

1 egg, beaten

1 tablespoon chopped parsley

500 grams fresh pasta, rolled thinly (see pp. 62–3)

Paolo's tomato sauce (p. 38)

Mix the ricotta in a bowl with a wooden spoon, adding in the ham, Parmesan, mozzarella, egg and parsley. Make small mounds of this mix on half your sheet of pasta at regular intervals, then fold the other half over that. Cut out the squares of ravioli, making sure the edges of each are tightly closed. Cook the ravioli in boiling salted water for 10 minutes. Transfer the ravioli to a bowl, cover them with tomato sauce and stir carefully to avoid breaking the ravioli. Serve with a sprinkle of Parmesan on top.

Spinach and Ricotta

This is a classic filling that turns up in many of the filled pasta shapes. Ricotta is what you make when you've finished making cheese, since it's made from whey. Strictly speaking it's not cheese, but is made from the milk solids. It's easy enough to find in shops these days, but if it interests you, I tell you how to make ricotta in the section on cheese-making later in the book (p. 176).

Prepare the spinach as described for the *cannelloni alla besciamella*, cooking it in as little water as possible. Chop or blend it finely and mix it with an equal quantity of ricotta. Season and fill the pasta as before.

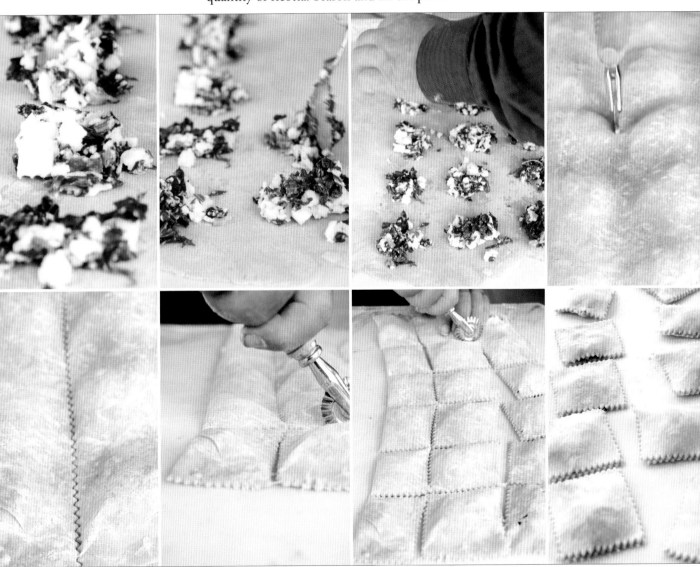

Oven-baked Pasta

The most common of all the oven-baked pastas are lasagne. These flat sheets of rolled pasta must be cooked before you assemble the dish. There are cookbooks that will tell you there's no need to do that, but trust me, there is. If you don't cook the lasagne first, all the starch from the pasta will remain in the finished dish, making it heavy and glutinous.

Boil some salted water in a wide tray deep enough to hold water and drop the lasagne into it one at a time. Cook them for 5 to 6 minutes and use a slotted spoon to remove them. After they're cooked, lay them on a damp tea towel to drain. Assemble the dish with these cooked sheets.

Lasagna Bolognese

This recipe uses the two base sauces, the *ragù alla Bolognese* (p. 40) and béchamel (p. 15).

Preheat the oven to 200°C and grease an ovenproof dish with butter. Cook your lasagne sheets in boiling salted water for 5 to 6 minutes and drain them on a damp tea towel. Put a layer of lasagne in the bottom of the greased dish. Cover it with a layer of the ragù, then a layer of béchamel. Sprinkle some freshly grated Parmesan over it and begin a new layer of lasagne. Repeat until you've used up all your sauces and lasagne. Finish up with a layer of béchamel and bake in the oven for half an hour.

Lasagna Napoletana

Preheat the oven to 160°C and grease an ovenproof dish. Make Paolo's tomato sauce (p. 38) and hard boil 4 eggs. Mix together 300 grams of mince, 1 beaten egg and some freshly grated Parmesan and form this mix into small meatballs. Shallow fry these in some olive oil over a medium heat and set them aside. Cook your lasagne in boiling salted water for 5 to 6 minutes and drain them on a damp tea towel. Put the first layer of lasagne in the greased dish. Spoon the tomato sauce over this, add some sliced boiled egg, cubes of mozzarella and meatballs. Repeat with more layers until you've used up all the ingredients, finishing with a layer of tomato sauce. Cover the dish with greased baking paper or foil and bake for about 1 hour.

Pasta al Forno — Baked Pasta

Lasagne are not the only form of pasta that is baked. In Italy, *pasta al forno* is very common and often it's done simply as a way to use up leftover pasta. Either way, the pasta is cooked and then reheated in the oven. *Pasta al forno* is a good dish for dinner parties in your own house, since it can be made in advance and it won't spoil if people are late arriving.

You can make it as you would a lasagna, alternating layers of pasta with tomato sauce and béchamel. You can make it with just a ragù or just béchamel — the choice is yours. Just make sure that whatever sauces you use are liquid enough so that the pasta won't dry out in the oven.

Mixing in cubes of mozzarella always goes down well, as the molten mozzarella makes those lovely gooey strings as you fork through the pasta. If you're going to use cubes of mozzarella, keep it to the inside, because if it's on the top, it will burn.

Timballo di Maccheroni — Timbale of Macaroni

I've left this recipe to the end, because it's a dish for special occasions and it does need a little bit of work, but what a reception it will receive when you produce it.

Begin by making a white sauce as per the recipe on p. 15 and a *ragù alla Bolognese* as per the recipe on p. 40.

An old-fashioned mixing bowl, carefully buttered on the inside, works quite well for this. First you need to find a pasta shape called bucatini, which are long, thin tubes. Cook 250 grams of this pasta and strain the pasta, keeping the hot water. When it's cool enough to handle, start by coiling one length at the bottom of the bowl. Work your way up and around the bowl, adding one length at a time, until you've reached the top or have run out of bucatini, whichever comes first. Plaster the pasta with some of the white sauce, which will hold it in place.

While you're doing this, cook 500 grams of penne in the boiling water you used for the bucatini. When the penne are cooked *al dente*, place some in the bottom of the bowl. Spoon a layer of ragù on top of that, then continue adding layers of penne, alternating the béchamel with the ragù until you've filled the bowl. Finish with a layer of béchamel.

Sit the bowl in a large pot of simmering water, making sure the water doesn't touch the bottom of the bowl, creating a bain-marie. Let the timbale heat slowly with a cover on it – about 45 minutes should heat it through. Carefully turn it out onto a serving plate, take it to the table and collect your praise.

Making Pasta

Like much of Italian cooking, making pasta isn't difficult, but it is very labour intensive. It's a great way to build up strong arm muscles. Maddalena Vacana, the mother of my good friend and poet Gerardo Vacana, was as adept a pasta maker as ever I came across. A small, wiry woman, she made the most silken pasta, a result of endless rolling, folding and rolling again until the pasta was almost translucent. She had her own technique of using a broom handle as a rolling pin. I've tried this and found it far too hard to manage — I could never stop the pasta rolling itself around the broom handle. I use a standard rolling pin and it works well for me.

Sieve 500 grams of flour onto a board or table and gather it into a small mound. Now make a well in the centre of the mound and break 4 eggs into this. Since humidity levels vary and egg sizes aren't constant, this is just the start. You may need to add a little water if the pasta gets too stiff or more flour if it's not stiff enough.

With your fingers, start working the flour into the eggs, and it will gradually form a paste. Now comes the hard work. Roll out the pasta as thin as you can. Fold it in half and then in half again and roll it out again. Keep doing this until you think your arms are about to give up. Trust me – the more you roll it, the better it will be.

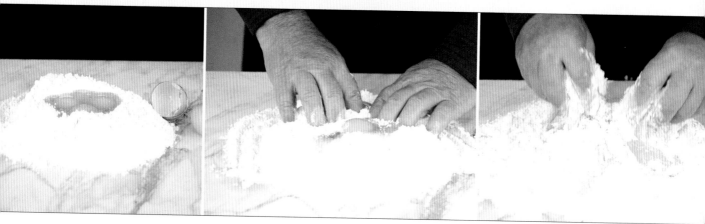

You can buy a simple little pasta maker, which looks for all the world like a miniature mangle. This is brilliant for rolling out the pasta, as you can set the rollers increasingly close together, giving you a delicate, fine pasta. Just as you do by hand, keep folding the pasta in half and passing it through the rollers over and over again.

You can do some fun things with this little machine, like putting sage leaves between the folds and then running it through the rollers. You'll end up with pasta with sage leaves inside it. You can experiment with this idea and try other herbs.

Once you have your thin sheets of silken pasta, you can start to cut it. Use a knife to cut it into thin strips for tagliatelle or into pieces about 10 centimetres by 5 centimetres for lasagne. You can also cut odd shapes, which are known as *maltagliate*, or *sagne* in my part of Italy. If you like the little nests of tagliatelle, then using plenty of flour as you go, roll your sheet up like a Swiss roll. Keep flouring as you roll, as you don't want the pasta to stick to itself. Then, with a sharp knife, cut across the roll, keeping each cut close to the edge, which will give you thin strips. When you've finished cutting, take 4 or 5 of these cut spirals and shake them loose so that you get a nest of tagliatelle that are not stuck together.

A chitarra

People who made a lot of their own pasta often had a device called a *chitarra*, which is the Italian for guitar. It's a simple frame with thin wires stretched across it and placed close to one another. You put your sheet of pasta on top of these wires and run a rolling pin over them, which then cut the pasta into strips. *Pasta alla chitarra* is made like this.

Fresh pasta cooks quickly – about 4 minutes.

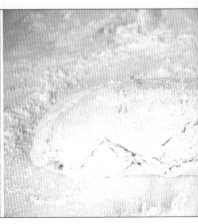

Gnocchi

Gnocchi, pronounced 'nyockey', are commonly eaten in place of pasta all over Italy. You can treat them exactly as you would pasta, but traditionally they're served with rich, heavy sauces.

Although the Tuscans make a spinach and ricotta dumpling which they call *gnocchi verdi*, usually gnocchi are made from potatoes. Mashed potato and flour are mixed together to make a paste hard enough to roll out like dough. The problem is this: the more flour you add, the easier it is to make the gnocchi, but the more they'll be like hard little bullets when cooked. Less flour makes the gnocchi far more palatable.

The secret to good gnocchi is in cooking the potatoes. The less moisture there is in the final mash, the less flour you will need. Waxy Italian potatoes work best, but any waxy potato that's steamed, rather than boiled, will produce good gnocchi. Microwaving the potatoes works well too.

Try not to let the potato to flour ratio go below four to one, for example roughly 250 grams of plain flour, but no more, to 1 kilo of potatoes.

You can add a little butter and 1 egg per 500 grams of potatoes, but if you have a runny mix it will make things worse.

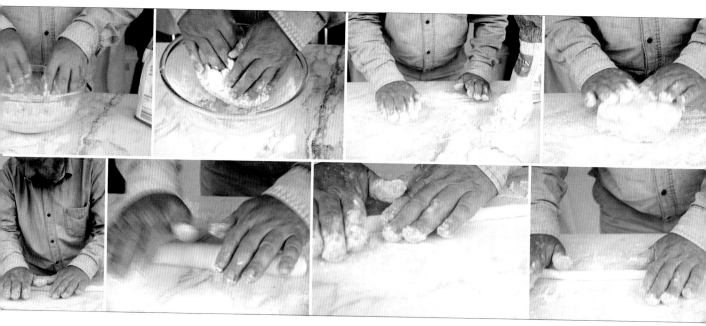

Salt the paste to taste. Roll out some of the paste on a board until you have a snake about the thickness of a finger. Cut this into roughly 5 centimetre-long pieces. Give each piece a squeeze in the middle to make it curl slightly. Cook the gnocchi by dropping them one at a time into boiling salted water. They will float to the top when they're cooked. As they cook, take them out of the pan with a slotted spoon and put them into a preheated ovenproof dish with a little butter.

Gnocchi in Bianco – Gnocchi in Butter

About as simple as you can get. Stir butter into the gnocchi and then grate on some Parmesan. That's it. This combination of butter and Parmesan works equally well with pasta (p. 34). Many children prefer this dish to all others.

Gnocchi alla Zia Rosa – Aunt Rosa's Gnocchi

My great aunt Rosa has gnocchi down to a fine art. I've never tasted better than hers. She is a traditionalist in this; she believes that gnocchi work best with a strong *sugo*, that is, a well boiled-down tomato sauce in which there is either pancetta or sausage. You could use streaky bacon, but you won't get the authentic Italian taste if you do.

Gnocchi alla Sorrentina –
GNOCCHI SORRENTO STYLE

This is a favourite from the Naples region, named after the town of Sorrento, where they make it using the buffalo mozzarella from that area.

Preheat the oven to 200°C. Cook your gnocchi in boiling salted water, then drain it and put it back in the pot. Stir in tomato sauce – use the *pizzaiola* recipe on p. 36. Thinly slice 250 grams of mozzarella and add it to the gnocchi. Give it a final stir, put it into an ovenproof dish and put it into the hot oven until the mozzarella has melted. Serve quickly.

Gnocchi di Ricotta e Spinaci –
SPINACH AND RICOTTA GNOCCHI

Although this dish uses the word 'gnocchi', in this case it's not made from potatoes.

Cook 1 kilo of spinach in a frying pan over a medium heat in only the water that remains on the leaves after washing it for about 5 minutes. Squeeze out as much liquid as you can after it's cooked. Chop it finely and mix it in a bowl with 350 grams of ricotta, 2 egg yolks and 2 tablespoons of freshly grated Parmesan. Season the mixture and shape it into balls about the size of golf balls. Drop them a few at a time into boiling salted water, and as soon as they rise to the top, they're cooked. Take them out with a slotted spoon and put them into a warm dish. When all the gnocchi are cooked, pour melted butter over them and sprinkle with 2 tablespoons of grated Parmesan before serving.

Polenta

While the northern Italians look down disdainfully at the southerners and call them *terroni*, or earth-grubbers, the southerners look at the northerners and call them *polentoni*, or polenta-bellies. The culinary differences are not what they once were, although the political ones remain, but traditionally, polenta — made from maize meal — was a northern dish.

illed maize was always a staple. Polenta is the same dish known in America's south as hominy grits. It's cheap, filling and versatile. Most cookbooks will tell you to pour the maize meal into already boiling water. This involves stirring fast while pouring to ensure no lumps form. I suggest you try an alternative – mixing the meal and cold water, then allowing it to come to the boil.

Whatever receptacle you use to measure the maize meal, add three times that same measurement of water and salt it. Stir it, and when it starts to boil, reduce the heat until the polenta plops quietly. Stir occasionally to ensure that it doesn't stick to the bottom. Polenta takes about half an hour to cook, so if it starts to look very dry, add a little more water. When it begins to separate from the edge of the pot, it's cooked.

Plain Polenta

Once it's cooked, you can prepare polenta the simplest way of all: add butter and freshly grated Parmesan and stir it in. You can serve it like this as a substitute for mashed potatoes.

Polenta with *Sugo*

Make Paolo's tomato sauce (p. 38) and add to it as many Italian sausages as there are people to feed. Let the sausages gently cook in the sauce for 15 minutes. While they cook, ladle the cooked polenta onto a board and spread it out until it's about 1 centimetre thick. Slice it into 8-centimetre or 10-centimetre squares. Put a square on a plate, 1 sausage and a ladle of tomato sauce. Top with freshly grated Parmesan.

Fried Polenta

Ladle the cooked polenta onto a board and spread it out until it's about 1 centimetre thick. Cut it into approximately 5-centimetre squares. Cover the bottom of a heavy frying pan with oil and heat it till it smokes. Dip each square of polenta into beaten egg and fry on both sides until crisp.

Baked Polenta

Oil the base of an ovenproof dish and add a layer of cooked polenta about 1 centimetre thick. Top this layer with some cooked mushrooms and onions, small cubes of mozzarella and a béchamel sauce (p. 15). Add another layer of polenta and repeat the process. Finally, top the last layer of polenta with freshly grated Parmesan. Put it in the hot oven for about half an hour – just long enough for the mozzarella to melt – and it's ready to eat. This is a dish that will hold well in a warm oven, so it can be prepared well in advance and left in a low oven until needed.

Polenta di Patate – Potato Polenta

Boil 1 kilo of potatoes until they're soft. Mash and season them, then gradually add 100 grams of polenta flour and 2 tablespoons of olive oil. Fry 200 grams of bacon in oil with 1 diced onion until cooked. Add this to the mashed potato mix with 200 grams of grated Pecorino cheese, or failing that, Parmesan. A little dried oregano works well in this dish. Now mould the mashed potato into a cake and put it under a grill to brown the top before serving.

Polenta con le Uova – Polenta with Eggs

Make 350 grams of polenta as described on p. 69, and as soon as it's ready, stir in 50 grams of butter. Poach 4 eggs and serve one per person on a bed of polenta. Runny yolks and polenta go together very nicely.

Rice Dishes

Risotto is Italian for a dish made with *riso*, the Italian for rice. There are as many recipes for risotto as there are towns in Italy, but some work better than others. Italians make their risotto with Italian rice, most often Arborio, although fancier varieties such as Carnaroli are available. They cook it by the gradual addition of stock to the rice as it cooks and absorbs liquid.

This is how northern Italians make their risotto. Start by warming your rice in oil, making sure all the grains are coated. Gradually add cupfuls of boiling stock – usually chicken stock – which you keep simmering in a pot alongside your risotto pot. As the rice cooks and absorbs the stock, you add more. The drawback to this method is that you're standing and stirring continually for 20 minutes, although the result if you're careful will be a beautifully creamy risotto.

There are many ways to cook rice, each suited to a particular dish. Let's start with plain white rice, cooked the Neapolitan way. Fill a large saucepan with water and bring it to the boil. Now salt it and add the rice – about 70 grams per person for a small helping, 100 grams for a large helping. Stir occasionally with a wooden spoon while the water bubbles vigorously. Between 15 and 18 minutes is about right for the cooking time, although just as with pasta, it's a good idea to start tasting from 15 minutes on to ensure the rice doesn't become over-cooked. It's exactly the same way we cook pasta. When it's ready, drain it through a sieve or fine colander. Put it into a heated, shallow dish and allow the rice to dry before serving.

Just like gnocchi and pasta, the addition of nothing more than butter and freshly grated Parmesan makes excellent eating. However, you can add whatever pleases you to the rice at this stage: tomato sauce, quartered boiled eggs, peas, fried mushrooms, meatballs, bacon, or in moments of wild abandon, white truffles.

A third and successful way of cooking rice is by the total absorption method. For 1 cup of rice use 3 cups of water or stock. Melt a knob of butter in a saucepan or pour in some olive oil and then put in the rice. Stir with a wooden spoon until all the grains are coated. Now add the water and stir once more. Let the water come to the boil, then turn down the heat to a simmer. When all the water has been absorbed, the rice is cooked.

The main difference between these ways of cooking rice is what happens to the starch in the rice. Using the Neapolitan way, the rice in the starch goes into the cooking water and is not present in the cooked rice once drained. In both of the other two ways, the starch remains in the rice, giving it a creamy consistency.

So, armed with three different ways of cooking rice, here are some classic recipes.

Risotto Rosso — Red Risotto

This is a good one to start with, since there's little that can go wrong. This recipe will feed six.

Start by making Paolo's tomato sauce as described on p. 38 and preheating the oven to 200°C. Put 500 grams of rice into a large pot of boiling water or stock and let it boil for 15 minutes. While it's cooking, hard boil 4 eggs and fry 4 slices of pancetta or rashers. Boil a cup of peas, which will add some colour to our risotto. Cut 250 grams of mozzarella into small cubes.

When the rice is done, strain it through a fine colander and put half of it into an ovenproof dish. Cover the top with half of the tomato sauce, the eggs cut into quarters, the pancetta, peas and half the mozzarella cubes, and if you like, some stoned black olives. Add the rest of the rice, the rest of the tomato sauce and the rest of the mozzarella and sprinkle the top with freshly grated Parmesan. Put the dish into the preheated oven for half an hour.

When my Aunt Gerardella used to make this, she'd also add *polpette*, or meatballs (p. 140), which makes this into quite a substantial dish. Done like Aunty did it, it becomes a one-plate meal.

Risotto ai Fungi – Mushroom Risotto

This is a real classic and it's a winner when it comes out right. In an ideal world, the mushrooms you'll use for this are what Italians call porcini and we call ceps or penny buns. These are perhaps the finest mushroom of all and they do grow in Ireland. Their botanical name is *boletus edulis*, and if you're lucky you'll find them growing in broad-leafed woods.

If foraging for mushrooms isn't for you, dried porcini can be bought in many delicatessens and good grocery stores. You can, of course, substitute other mushrooms, but if you do, avoid using button mushrooms, as they're almost devoid of flavour.

If you're using dried porcini, they need to be rehydrated. Put them in a bowl with some tepid water and let them slowly reabsorb the water. This time we'll make the risotto using the 'little at a time' method.

You'll need a pot in which you'll make the risotto and another for the simmering vegetable stock. Melt a knob of butter in the risotto pot and add 100 grams of rice per person, which makes a generous portion. Coat the rice in the melted butter, turning it with a wooden spoon. Add a cupful of stock and turn up the heat. You can now add the mushrooms. If you're using dried ones that you've soaked, use the water that they've been soaking in, it will have a strong mushroom taste. It's a good idea to strain this water through a fine sieve, as dried mushrooms often have little grains of sand on them, and we don't want that in the risotto.

You must be patient now – you can't go off and do something else, you have to stand next to your risotto and watch it. As the rice starts to absorb your stock, you must add more, always a little at a time. After about 15 minutes, start to taste the rice. You don't want it to be soggy, but there's nothing worse than undercooked rice. A bit of tooth resistance is good, but don't overdo the *al dente*. You want to end up with a creamy risotto, not a dry one.

Salting anything with mushrooms needs care. They absorb salt quite willingly, so taste your risotto before you serve it, making sure there's enough salt. If you want some added smoothness, add butter. Butter and risottos go well together, but don't go overboard.

Risotto Milanese

This is a risotto that you can make by the total absorption method. Allow 100 grams of rice per person. A good idea is to put the rice into a measuring jug and take note of what level the rice came to. Cover the bottom of a pan with some olive oil and pour in the rice, turning it in the oil until all the grains are coated. Now fill the jug to the same level as the rice was with vegetable stock and pour that over your rice. Now turn up the heat. Add another 2 jugfuls to the rice and keep a fourth jug ready, which you might or might not need.

Now's the time to put your saffron into the pot. Saffron costs more than gold by weight, so it's not something we throw around. The good news is that you don't need much of it to give your risotto a fabulous yellow colour and the aroma of saffron. A big pinch between the thumb and forefinger is plenty.

Stir your risotto from time to time, until you notice that there's no more liquid on the top of it. Now you have to start tasting it. It it's still hard, then you'll need some of the fourth jug of stock that you've kept back. Use enough stock to make sure the rice is cooked.

Turn off the heat and stir in a large dollop of butter. How much you use is up to you; I use a lot. Stir in some freshly grated Parmesan and put the lid on the pot. A refinement is to add beef bone marrow. Let it sit for 5 minutes before serving.

Supplì – Rice Balls

One of my favourite rice dishes is *supplì*. They're rice balls and they can be very simple or, in the case of Sicilian *arancini*, very complex. To make them you'll need to cook the rice a little longer than you normally do so that the rice becomes soft rather than *al dente*.

Cook 250 grams of rice, and as soon as it's cool enough to handle, mix the rice with 2 egg yolks and 100 grams of freshly grated Parmesan. Roll the rice into balls about the size of a tangerine, then roll them in seasoned flour, then in beaten egg, then in breadcrumbs. Shallow fry them until they're golden and serve them as an accompaniment in place of plain rice or potatoes.

You can make a fancier version, which is called *supplì al telefono* in Italy. This reference to telephones is in fact to telephone wires, because you place a cube of mozzarella inside each rice ball, and when you cut into the cooked *supplì*, the melted mozzarella will form strings as you pull the *supplì* apart, just like telephone wires.

Pizza

One of the joys of starting a kitchen from scratch is that you can fill the bare walls with exactly the kitchen you want. I was lucky enough to be able to do this in my last house, so apart from the obvious culinary necessities, pride of place was taken up with my brick-domed wood-fired pizza oven. I call it a pizza oven, but it was no different from the ovens built in Anatolia 5,000 years ago. A design this old and used in so many cultures is obviously a versatile one; apart from pizza, it can cook anything else, as any oven would. But I didn't build it to replace my gas oven — I made it specifically for pizza and bread.

Friends were quick to demand pizza nights, and at first I was happy to oblige, eager to show off. But here's the rub: it's hard work. While everyone eats and at times compliments the pizza, the cook stands sweating at the oven door, paddle in hand. By the time it was finally my turn, the fillings seemed to have gone, the fire was no longer at its best and everyone else was onto the coffee and fags.

When I was a small boy, there was an oven just like mine in the kitchen of the family house in Italy, and just like mine it was built into a corner next to the hearth. Once a week, on a Monday, my grandmother would bake eight large *pagnotte*, round 2-kilo loaves that would be kept, wrapped in linen, in a large wooden chest. These were sourdough loaves, every week she'd keep back a small piece of dough and add a little sugar and water to it. The yeast in the dough would multiply and this would become the starter yeast for the next week's baking.

By the following Sunday what bread was left would be rock hard and edible only after soaking a slice in milk or wine. When the bread baking was over, *Nonna* would make pizza with the dough that was left. She would stoke the oven once more to get the heat up and occasionally check the temperature with a piece of newspaper. If it went brown and curled up, she knew the temperature was over 400°F; if it burst into flame, then the temperature was over 450°F, hot enough to cook a pizza in 4 or 5 minutes.

Pizza for me and mine has a thin base and is made with yeast, strong flour, water and, when cooked in a domestic oven, a little olive oil. The variations on this recipe available in Ireland may be good pies, but they are not pizzas. For me, pizza is Neapolitan; the closer it conforms to that ideal, the more I like it. The classic Neapolitan pizza recipe is this: for 500 grams of strong flour you need 2 teaspoons of salt, 30 grams of fresh yeast or its dry equivalent, a pinch of sugar, 1 tablespoon of good olive oil and enough water to make a firm dough, approximately 250 ml. This will make four roughly 25-centimetre pizzas.

Mix the flour and salt in a mixing bowl. Meanwhile, add the fresh yeast to a glass of warm water with a pinch of sugar and stir it well with a fork. For dried yeast, follow the instructions on the packet. When the yeast is foamy and creamy, make a well in the flour and add the yeast and the olive oil. Start making the dough by adding the water a little at a time until the dough is firm and well mixed. Knead the dough until it's silky and elastic, then put it in a floured bowl, cover with a plastic bag or damp tea towel and leave to rise in a warm place. A cross cut on the top will help. When it has risen, which depending on the room temperature will be between 1 and 3 hours, knock the dough back by kneading it again. Now roll out your 4 pizzas. Put them on oiled tins or trays and ladle on your *pizzaiola* sauce (p. 36).

Pizza needs a hot oven, preheated to about 220°C or 425°F. Between 5 and 10 minutes should be sufficient, depending on the topping.

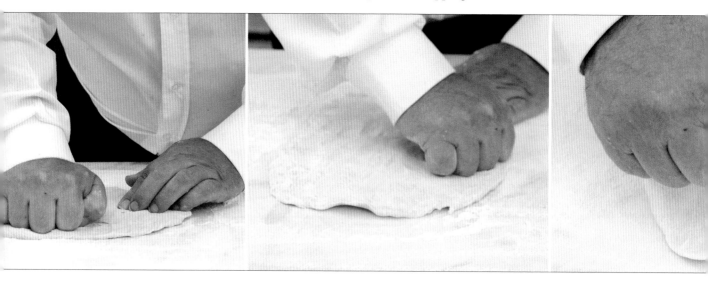

A dish of boiling water in the oven will help give a crusty texture to the dough. I like to give a pizza two passes in the oven, which is a way of ensuring you won't have a topping of burnt mozzarella. Put the pizza in the first time with just the tomato sauce and olive oil on it, until the base is almost cooked. Remove it and add the mozzarella and whatever other topping you want, then put it back in the oven to finish it off.

If you want to be as authentic as possible, use San Marzano tomatoes for the tomato sauce – they're the ones they use in Naples. If you can find buffalo mozzarella, use that rather than the cows' milk one. Mozzarella is a cheese that needs to be very fresh – the fresher, the better. Any mozzarella that's been in a plastic packet for three weeks isn't going to taste anything like a fresh one.

Don't use the pizza as a dumping ground for things found lurking in the back of the fridge – stick with some classic toppings which have proved their appeal over the years. A simple *Margherita* – tomato sauce, mozzarella and leaves of basil – is hard to beat. Although you can find pizzas with pineapple and sweetcorn outside of Italy, these are not generally accepted as pizza toppings by Italians. You can be inventive and use many things, but if you want to strive for authenticity, avoid pineapple and sweetcorn. There's no harm in being experimental, but the classic pizza recipes have become classics over the centuries because they work so well. There's no need to reinvent the wheel.

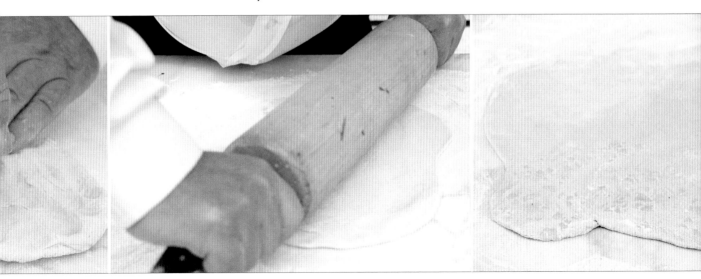

THE FARINACEOUS DISHES

Margherita

This topping has a special place in Italy. It was created in Naples especially for the new queen of Italy, Margherita, the wife of Victor Emmanuel. It uses the colours of the Italian flag, red, white and green. The red is the tomato sauce, the white is the mozzarella and the green is leaves of basil. Simple, tasty and classic.

Marinara

The name might lead you to think that this pizza uses seafood, but it's actually named after the wives of the fishermen who used to make it. The *marinara* and the *Margherita* are the only two pizzas whose toppings are codified by the Authentic Pizza Association of Naples. For this pizza, you'll need only *pizzaiola* sauce (p. 36), garlic, oregano and olive oil.

Capricciosa

Literally a 'capricious' pizza, this is the one I nearly always order when I'm in an Italian pizzeria. As always, the base is covered with tomato sauce and the topping is made up of mozzarella, mushrooms, artichoke hearts, cooked ham and stoned olives. In Lazio, you'll often find half a hard-boiled egg in the middle.

Quattro Stagioni

This is a common pizza whose name means 'four seasons', so called because the topping is divided into quarters. The ingredients are exactly the same as the *capricciosa*, they're just arranged differently on the crust.

Frutta di Mare

There are no hard and fast rules for this pizza topping, but it's true that seafood goes very well on top of a pizza. Cover your pizza with the *pizzaiola* sauce (p. 36), then a layer of clams, mussels, shrimp and baby squid and top it off with olive oil.

Calzone

There are many varieties of fillings for a calzone, which is basically a pizza folded in half and filled before baking. Mix together 50 grams of mozzarella chopped small with 30 grams of diced Italian salami, 30 grams of cooked, diced ham and 30 grams of ricotta. Fill only half the pizza round and fold over the other half, crimping the edges carefully. Bake it as you would a pizza, but let it cook for 15 minutes.

Potato Pizza

In Italy, you can find pizzerias called *pizza al taglio*, which means pizza by the slice. It's a kind of fast food take-away. Inside you'll find large trays of pizzas, rather than individual ones. You buy it by the *etto*, the 100-gram measure. Apart from the *marinara* and the *Margherita*, you'll often find a potato pizza.

This pizza requires a double pass in the oven. First, boil a few potatoes for 15 minutes, then slice thinly. Cover the pizza dough with the sliced potato and cook for 15 minutes. Take it out of the oven and cover the potato layer with diced pancetta, shavings of Parmesan and diced Taleggio cheese. Drizzle the top with olive oil and sprinkle with chopped rosemary. Now put it back in the oven for between 5 and 8 minutes before serving.

Bread

Good bread is an asset to any table. There is nothing as basic to our diet as a loaf — it can accompany virtually any food and is filling and versatile. But occasionally a fancy bread can make a welcome change. These breads can be bought increasingly easily, but some are extraordinarily easy to make at home.

Making bread at home satisfies an atavistic urge to get back to basics. Somehow a hot loaf from the oven, its smell deeply redolent of times past, elicits images of traditional homesteads and simpler lives. Yet there is no mystery to its production, no cabalistic formulae, no alchemical arcana. The process is as simple and as traditional as the memories it evokes.

My mother taught me to make three savoury breads: tomato, olive and onion. All three are made in the same way, only the flavouring changes.

The recipe for the basic bread is this. For 450 grams of flour you'll need roughly 300 ml of tepid water, 30 grams of fresh yeast, a pinch of sugar, 1 teaspoon of salt and 1 tablespoon of olive oil. Fresh yeast can be found at most bakeries and supermarkets. You can, of course, use the equivalent amount of dried yeast, but it can give different results.

Pour some of the water into a glass and add the yeast and the pinch of sugar. Stir well until it dissolves and wait till it froths. Put the flour into a mixing bowl. Add the salt, olive oil, the dissolved yeast and most of the tepid water. Mix well, and if necessary add the rest of the water to make a firm but pliable dough.

For tomato bread, at the mixing stage add a 140-gram tin of tomato purée and a little chopped or dried basil, then proceed as above. For olive bread, add 140 grams of tapenade (p. 20) and, optionally, some chopped olives. For onion bread, add a medium onion that's been diced small and sweated in olive oil. A little turmeric improves the colour.

Leave the dough at room temperature overnight. Knock it back in the morning and put it into a greased loaf tin. Let it rise again to fill the tin and preheat the oven to 220°C. Bake for 40 to 45 minutes. Don't be surprised if the onion bread rises more than the other two; I have no idea why it should, but it does.

Primi Piatti –
First Courses

The most common of all first courses in Italy is, of course, pasta, but in this chapter we'll deal with first courses that are not pasta, gnocchi, polenta or rice.

Soups

Soups are obvious candidates for this section, so we'll start with them. The Italian word for soup is *minestra*, so a big soup is a *minestrone*. There are many recipes for minestrone, but all of them have these things in common — garden vegetables, rice, pasta or pulses and olive oil or bacon fat.

Minestrone alla Milanese

olive oil

50 grams bacon lardons

½ onion, chopped

½ garlic clove, chopped

3 tomatoes, chopped

3 potatoes, chopped

2 carrots, chopped

2 courgettes, sliced

1 stick of celery

100 grams cannellini beans

salt and freshly ground black
  pepper

½ cabbage, shredded – I like to
  use Savoy cabbage

200 grams peas

100 grams long-grained rice or
  ditalini

chopped fresh sage, to serve

chopped fresh basil, to serve

freshly grated Parmesan,
  to serve

Heat some olive oil in a pot over a medium heat. Shallow fry the lardons with the onion and garlic. When the fat runs from the lardons, add the tomatoes, potatoes, carrots, courgettes, celery, cannellini, 2 tablespoons of olive oil and 3 litres of water. Season and bring to the boil, then lower the heat to a gentle simmer and leave it to cook for 2 hours. Lastly, add the cabbage, peas and rice and cook for another 20 minutes, stirring from time to time. Just before serving, stir in the chopped sage and basil and sprinkle the top with freshly grated Parmesan.

Minestrone d'Inverno — WINTER MINESTRONE

My cousin Gigino's wife, Liliana, used to make a wonderful minestrone using winter vegetables. In our part of Italy it was normal to put a slice or two of stale bread at the bottom of the soup bowl before putting in the soup. It was a way of using up stale bread and it added to the soup's nourishment.

5 chard stems
2 potatoes
2 carrots
2 leeks
1 small cabbage
1 turnip
1 stick of celery
1 ham bone
freshly grated Parmesan,
  to serve

Chop all the vegetables into small pieces and put into a pot with 2 litres of water and a pinch of salt. Traditionally there would also be a ham bone in the soup, but some chopped-up Italian sausage or even some chopped chorizo could take its place. Bring it to the boil, then lower the heat to a gentle simmer. Cook for 1 hour, then take a cupful of the soup and blend it till smooth before returning it to the pot. If the idea of stale bread in the bottom of the bowl doesn't appeal to you, you can add carbohydrates by using small pasta shapes like ditalini and leave the soup on the heat until the pasta is cooked. Serve with a sprinkling of freshly grated Parmesan.

Minestrone alla Napoletana — NEAPOLITAN MINESTRONE

My friend Maria Franciosa is well known for her cooking on Neapolitan TV. She's as glamorous as Sofia Loren, and like Sofia, she loves living in Naples. She taught me a lot about Neapolitan cooking and this is one of her recipes.

1 yellow pepper
50 grams pancetta, diced
olive oil
½ onion, chopped
½ carrot, chopped
1 garlic clove, chopped
3 tomatoes, chopped

salt and freshly ground black
  pepper
2 aubergines, chopped
2 potatoes, chopped
2 courgettes, chopped
1 head of endive, cut into thin
  strips

½ small cabbage, shredded
100 grams peas
100 grams ditalini pasta
chopped fresh basil, to serve
freshly grated Parmesan, to
  serve

Cook the pepper as described on pp. 25–6. Fry the pancetta in oil over a medium heat with the onion, carrot and garlic. Add the tomatoes and cook for 15 minutes. Add 2 litres of water and seasoning. Bring it to the boil, then add the cooked yellow pepper, aubergines, potatoes, courgettes, endive, cabbage and peas. Let this simmer for another half an hour. Lastly, add the ditalini and cook for another 10 minutes or so, until the pasta is cooked. Sprinkle it with basil and Parmesan before serving.

Minestra ai Fiori di Zucchini – COURGETTE FLOWER SOUP

It's worth growing your own courgettes just so you can have courgette flowers. They're delicious deep fried in batter, but they also make a good soup.

Make 1 litre of meat stock, either the hard way or with bought stock cubes, and bring it to the boil. Fry 1 chopped onion and 1 chopped carrot with 1 grated celery stick on a low heat for 10 minutes. Add 4 sliced courgettes and 20 sliced courgette flowers and cook for 2 minutes. Lastly, add 120 grams of small pasta, such as ditalini, and cook until it's *al dente*. Season and serve with a sprinkling of freshly grated Parmesan.

Gazpacho

The word '*gazpacho*' is Spanish, but cold tomato soup isn't just the preserve of Spaniards.

Peel and slice 1 cucumber, salt it and leave it to drain in a colander. If you want to use up garden produce, take 1.5 kilos of fresh tomatoes and put them in a blender until they're liquidised. Alternatively, if you have no fresh tomatoes, use 1 litre of passata. Add the salted, drained cucumber, rinsing it first, then a couple of chopped spring onions, some chopped basil leaves and some chopped parsley. If you like garlic, stir in some puréed garlic cloves to your soup. Lastly, mix together 3 tablespoons of olive oil with the juice of 1 lemon and stir it into the soup. Refrigerate it for a few hours before serving.

Minestra di Ortiche – NETTLE SOUP

This a soup that I served often in my restaurant in the springtime, and I always thought of it as an Irish soup until I had it in Rome. There was a difference – the Roman version had pancetta in it.

Collect about half a kilo of nettles – gloves would be a good idea, and don't pick them from underneath rookeries. Pick the young shoots, not the hard old leaves. Wash and drain them.

Make 1 litre of chicken stock using cubes or a chicken carcass and bring it to the boil. Meanwhile, shallow fry 50 grams of pancetta with 1 crushed clove of garlic in a pot over a medium heat, then add 2 chopped tomatoes and cook for 10 minutes. Season, then add the nettles, letting them cook for 10 minutes. Lastly, add the stock and let the soup simmer for a few moments before serving.

Alternatively, boil the nettles in the stock for 10 minutes and use a stick blender to purée them before adding in the pancetta and tomatoes. Garnish with a nettle leaf that you've blanched in boiling water to remove the sting.

Risi e Bisi – Rice and Peas

This is one of the classic dishes that knows no regional boundaries; it's eaten all over Italy. It's a kind of halfway house between a risotto and a soup.

Start by making 1 litre of chicken stock using cubes or a chicken carcass and bring it to the boil.

Shallow fry a chopped onion, a grated stick of celery and a crushed clove of garlic in olive oil over a medium heat until the onion is translucent. Add 250 grams of peas and 200 grams of rice, either Arborio or Carnaroli, and stir together for 1 minute. Start adding the stock, a cupful at a time, until the rice is cooked and all the stock is used up.

Finish the soup by stirring in 50 grams of butter, 30 grams of freshly grated Parmesan and salt to taste.

Stracciatella

This is a soup I remember from my childhood, as it was one of Grandma's specialities. It's warming and filling.

Start by bringing 1.5 litres of chicken stock to the boil. Meanwhile, mix 30 grams of freshly grated Parmesan and 30 grams of breadcrumbs together with 3 beaten eggs in a bowl. Take a cupful of the warm stock and add it to the egg mixture, beating it until it's a smooth mixture.

When the stock is boiling, add the egg mixture, which will almost immediately float to the top. Break it up with a knife or fork, then serve the soup garnished with chopped parsley.

Two Quick Cheese Snacks

Here are two dishes that come in handy for a quick snack.

Crespelle di Formaggio e Prosciutto – CHEESE AND PROSCIUTTO PANCAKES

Preheat the oven to 200°C. Beat 2 eggs, 250 ml of milk and about 100 grams of plain flour to make a simple batter. Let it stand for a while. Warm a non-stick frying pan, or use a dab of butter, and spoon the batter into the pan, making sure it covers the whole of the base. When the top looks dry, turn the pancake over. Continue making pancakes until you've used up the batter.

Put a slice of prosciutto on a pancake and then a slice of cheese. Gruyère works well, but use the cheese of your choice. Now roll up the pancake and put it in an ovenproof dish, lining up the other filled pancakes alongside as you make them. When you've finished filling the pancakes, cover them with béchamel (p. 15). Check for seasoning, then put the dish in the oven for 20 minutes.

Mozzarella in Carozza – MOZZARELLA IN A CHARIOT

This is one of those great dishes that's really easy, perfectly delicious and that always impresses.

Beat 2 eggs in a soup bowl and season with salt and freshly ground black pepper. If you want to be refined, cut the crusts off 4 slices of bread and make 2 mozzarella sandwiches, pressing the sandwich together well. If the mozzarella is unsalted, sprinkle it with salt before closing the sandwich. Put your sandwiches in the beaten egg and let them stand long enough to absorb the egg, turning them once.

Shallow fry the sandwiches over a medium heat until the outside is golden and the mozzarella inside has started to melt. Serve quickly, so that the mozzarella is still runny when served.

Soufflés

Soufflé di Formaggio – Cheese Soufflé

The base of all souffles is béchamel sauce (p. 15). Make half a litre of white sauce and season it with salt and a little freshly grated nutmeg. Preheat the oven to 200°C.

To make this you'll need a bain-marie or a double boiler. You can do this easily by placing a bowl in a saucepan that has a little gently simmering water at the bottom of it. This ensures that the bowl is quite warm, but nowhere near boiling water temperature.

Put the béchamel into the bowl and stir in 4 egg yolks (save the whites). Add 150 grams of diced Emmental cheese and some freshly grated Parmesan too if you like and stir until the cheese has melted. You can use Grana Padana instead of Emmental, which also works well. Season it and let it cool down. Now beat the egg whites until they're stiff – they are what will give your soufflé lightness.

Gently fold the beaten egg whites into the cheese mixture – you don't want to lose those tiny bubbles of air. When it's well incorporated, pour the mixture into ramekins, filling each one two-thirds full. Put the ramekins into a roasting tray and fill the tray with water to half the ramekins' height. Bake them for 20 minutes or so, or until you see the soufflés rise. Serve them quickly in the ramekins, as soufflés collapse fast.

Soufflé di Pomodoro – Tomato Soufflé

Here's an opportunity to combine two base sauces, béchamel (p. 15) and Paolo's tomato sauce (p. 38). You'll need 500 ml of béchamel and 250 ml of tomato sauce, but this time don't add any olive oil to the reduced passata. Mix these sauces together and season, then stir in 4 egg yolks.

Whisk the 4 egg whites until they're very stiff and gently fold the stiffened whites into the mixture until it's well incorporated. Proceed as in the recipe on p. 91, cooking the soufflés for 20 minutes.

Egg Dishes

Uova in Purgatorio – Eggs in Purgatory

This is the first dish my mother taught me to make as a small boy. It's a fancy version of fried eggs, which in Italy is cooked and served in a *tegamino*, a small frying pan with two handles. My friend Laurent Mellet calls it 'eggs al Dante'.

Take 2 fresh farmyard eggs and fry them in good olive oil. As soon as the whites have set, spoon some tomato sauce over the eggs. Cook until the tomato sauce is heated through. Sprinkle with freshly grated Parmesan, then serve it with crusty bread, which is what you'll use to eat it with, using the crusts as spoons.

Uova con Pomodori – Tomato Eggs

Preheat the oven to 180°C. Cut off the tops of 4 tomatoes. Scoop out the seeds and some of the flesh, then sprinkle the insides with salt and freshly ground black pepper. Turn them upside down and let them drain for about 10 minutes. When they're drained, add a little oregano to each tomato and a dash of olive oil. Bake them in an ovenproof dish for 20 minutes.

Take the dish from the oven and break an egg into each tomato, then return the dish to the oven for another 5 minutes, or until the eggs are cooked. Garnish them with a sprig of basil and serve.

Uova Sode alla Napoletana –
NEAPOLITAN-STYLE BOILED EGGS

Hard boil 8 eggs and shell them. Cut them in half and remove the yolks, putting them into a bowl. Peel and deseed 4 tomatoes, then dice the flesh. Mash the egg yolks with 4 anchovy fillets, 30 grams of stoned olives, 1 tablespoon of diced tomato and enough mayonnaise to combine all the elements.

Now fill the halves of the boiled eggs with this mixture, heaping it well up on each half. Serve 4 per person, laying them on a bed of salad leaves and surrounding the eggs with the remaining tomatoes.

Uova Strapazzate al Tartufo –
SCRAMBLED EGGS WITH TRUFFLES

Truffles are a wonderful fungus with a dark, deep taste that grows on you the more you eat them. You may have heard of the white truffle of Alba, which can sell for up to €5,000 a kilo. I'll assume for this recipe that you don't have those. However, the black truffle, and there are two kinds, are much cheaper. There's the winter truffle and the summer truffle, which describes the time of year in which they're found. Of the two, the summer truffle is the cheapest, and in my opinion it's worth every cent. During the summer these can be bought for around €120 a kilo, but you don't need much to flavour a dish – €10 buys you quite enough.

They cost more in Ireland, but even if you can't find fresh truffles, you can find jars of truffle paste. These jars contain the broken truffles that were too small to sell and a fair percentage of ordinary mushrooms. Still, you do get the truffle taste. Bear in mind that truffle oil is not made from truffles – it's an oil flavoured with a chemical extract from whey that tastes just like truffle.

Eggs and truffles are perfect bedfellows. Eggs are good at absorbing flavours, so whisk 6 eggs in a bowl and stir in 2 teaspoons of truffle paste. Cover the bowl and leave it in the fridge overnight. If you don't cover it, everything in your fridge will smell of truffles.

The next morning, make 4 pieces of toast and butter them, then scramble your eggs and top the toast with them.

Uova Strapazzate nel Nido –
EGGS IN A NEST

I promise you this sounds harder than it actually is. Grate 2 peeled potatoes and squeeze as much liquid out of them as you can. Arrange some of the potato around the bottom and up the sides of a small sieve until you've made a thin dish shape. Now open up a small hole at the bottom so you can see the sieve's mesh.

Heat a small pot of frying oil until it's hot. Test it by placing slivers of potato in – if they immediately fizz, then the oil's hot enough. Now gently lower the sieve into the hot oil. The hole in the bottom will allow the hot oil to rise through the sieve and cook the inside of the potatoes. If you don't make a hole, the potato will float away from the sieve.

When the potato is golden brown, tip it out of the sieve onto kitchen paper to drain and you have your first potato basket. Cook 3 more baskets and use them to serve your scrambled eggs in. I love to serve truffled eggs like this.

Frittate – Omelettes

Omelettes are as common in Italy as they are elsewhere and are made with all the various fillings that you'd expect. Here are a couple of variations that are both interesting and good.

Frittata Ripiena – FILLED OMELETTE

Preheat the oven to 180°C. Beat 4 eggs with a little salt and freshly ground black pepper and pour the mix into a large frying pan or skillet to make a thin omelette. Cook it on both sides. Meanwhile, cook 200 grams of mushrooms in a small pot for 10 minutes over a medium heat. When they're cooked, add 50 grams of chopped ham and 50 grams of a cheese like Gruyère and take it off the heat.

Put this mixture on half of the omelette, fold it over and put it in the oven for a couple of minutes, until the cheese has melted, before serving.

Torta di Frittata – OMELETTE CAKE

The idea here is that you'll make three 2-egg omelettes, which you'll assemble into a cake. You can make each omelette with anything you care to use, but this particular combination works well and uses all the classic ingredients of the Italian kitchen.

Beat 2 eggs and season with salt and freshly ground black pepper. Pour this into your omelette pan and add a little chopped parsley. When it's still a little soft on top, slide it out of the pan and set it aside. Make 2 more omelettes the same way, but add freshly grated Parmesan to the third omelette.

Put your first omelette into a cake tin lined with greaseproof paper. Top it with slices of roasted aubergines and either Fontina or mozzarella cheese. Place the second omelette on top of that and cover that one with strips of roasted peppers and cheese. Lastly, place the third omelette soft side down on the top. You can serve this hot or cold. If hot, then bake it at 180°C for 10 minutes or so.

You can buy roasted aubergines and peppers in jars in most supermarkets, but if you want to do it yourself, here's how. Cut the aubergines into slices about 5 mm thick, either across or lengthways, and salt them well. Put them in a colander and let them drain for half an hour, then cook them on a hot griddle pan until they're golden brown on each side. You can cook the peppers as per the recipe on pp. 25–6.

Vegetables

The Italian kitchen makes use of an abundance of vegetables. This isn't surprising, given that Italy has been described as 'the garden of Europe'. In any Italian market, you'll find yourself confronted with a bewildering variety of vegetables, beautifully stacked to show them off to their best advantage. Boxes of tomatoes of all varieties, green vegetables in every conceivable shade and shape, pulses, beans and fruits are all displayed, their very abundance bringing on the first pangs of hunger.

PAOLO TULLIO COOKS ITALIAN

Many vegetables are eaten raw and most meals end with fresh fruit. Salads are much used, but in Italy salads are always served dressed. In Italy, dressing a salad does not need the careful measuring of ingredients to create a vinaigrette. Instead, the emphasis is always on the quality of two of the main ingredients, the olive oil and vinegar. These are poured and never measured. The third ingredient, salt, is rarely discussed.

Oil for salads is always of the highest quality, because once olive oil is heated, it loses its fresh taste. That freshness is what is needed when the oil is eaten uncooked. A good, well-aged vinegar – and always a wine vinegar – completes a salad dressing. First you salt the leaves, then you add the olive oil, then lastly the vinegar and toss the salad. A little practice is all you need to gauge the quantities, and from then on you'll dress your salads without a second thought.

Olive oil is rated by its acidity, that is, the amount of oleic acid that it contains. The less oleic acid, the better the oil. Extra virgin olive oil is defined as having less than 1 per cent oleic acid. If you read the back label, you'll rarely find an oil with much less acidity than that, simply because there's no benefit to the producer to lower the acidity below 1 per cent. In fact, if a batch of oil comes out with an acidity of, say, half a percent, most producers will add a lesser-quality oil until the acidity level is just below the magic 1 per cent mark. If you ever find an oil with a very low acidity level, keep it for salad dressing.

There's a technique that's worth learning that's frequently used for vegetables in Italy. It's called *ripassato in padella*, which translates as 'recooked in the pan'. What it means is that previously boiled vegetables, like turnip tops, are tossed in a pan with crushed garlic and olive oil. Even dull vegetables come to life when given this treatment.

Curiously, Italians are very fond of turnip tops, called *rape*. In Italy, the tops are harvested and sold in the markets, then the sheep get to eat the turnips. In Ireland, exactly the reverse applies – sheep are turned into turnip fields and are allowed to eat the tops, then the turnips are taken to market.

Many vegetables are delicious *ripassato in padella*. Spinach, sprouting broccoli, green beans – just about any leftover vegetables can be given a new lease of life when cooked this simple way.

Aubergines

Of all the common vegetables in Italy, the aubergine is the prince. It's versatile, beautiful to look at and tastes good.

Once upon a time it was common to slice aubergines, salt them and leave them to drain. With some of the older varieties this was essential, as they produced bitter juices that were removed by salting. Modern varieties have had those bitter juices bred out of them, but salting still has a purpose. By removing some of the water content, the flavours are intensified and many claim that aubergines will absorb less oil when they cook after salting. I've chosen these recipes to show the versatility of aubergines.

Caviale di Melanzane –
AUBERGINE CAVIAR

Cut off the tops and tails of 2 large or 3 medium aubergines and cook them in boiling salted water for about 15 minutes, or until they're soft. Drain them in a colander and leave them to lose as much water as possible.

Now skin them and mash the flesh with a fork, a potato masher or a blender. Flavour the purée with salt, pepper, the juice of a lemon and add about a wineglassful of olive oil, stirring until it's all blended. You can serve this as a side dish or on toasted bread as *crostini*.

Melanzane Arrosto –
ROASTED AUBERGINES

This is probably the commonest way of being presented with aubergines in Italy. Cut the aubergines into slices, either across or lengthways, depending on your preference, salt them and leave them to drain in a colander for half an hour or so.

Lay the slices on a baking tray and grill them for a few minutes on each side. Put a layer of the grilled aubergine slices on the bottom of an ovenproof dish, sprinkle with salt, pepper and a little crushed garlic, then drizzle with olive oil. Add another layer of aubergines and repeat until you've used up all the slices.

Put the dish in the fridge for at least 1 hour, as this allows all the flavours to blend together. Serve it cold as a side dish.

Melanzane Ripiene – STUFFED AUBERGINES

Preheat the oven to 200°C. Cut 4 small aubergines in half lengthways and scoop out as much of the flesh as you can, leaving the skin intact. Chop the flesh finely and mix 200 grams of diced mozzarella and a couple of anchovy fillets with it. Season the mix and add a splash of olive oil to it.

Divide the mixture into the 8 aubergine halves, topping each one with a spoonful of Paolo's tomato sauce (p. 38). Put the stuffed aubergines onto a baking tray and cook in the oven for about half an hour. Before serving, sprinkle the tops with some chopped basil.

Parmigiana di Melanzane – AUBERGINE *PARMIGIANA*

The *Parmigiana* is a classic dish and it's not confined to any one region of Italy. It's a dish you'll often see on menus in Ireland, but in my experience it's rarely done properly. It's not a difficult dish, it just needs a little preparation time.

Start by cutting 2 large or 4 small aubergines into slices, either across or lengthways, depending on your preference. Salt them and leave them to drain in a colander for half an hour or so. Make Paolo's tomato sauce as per the recipe on p. 38. Preheat the oven to 180°C.

Fry the aubergine slices in batches in olive oil on a medium heat until browned on both sides. Set them aside to drain on kitchen paper as you cook them. Meanwhile, beat 2 eggs and slice 100 grams of mozzarella thinly.

Assemble the *Parmigiana* by spooning a little tomato sauce into the bottom of an ovenproof dish, then add a layer of aubergine slices. Pour a little of the beaten egg over it, sprinkle it with freshly grated Parmesan and put a few slices of mozzarella around the top of the first layer, along with a few basil leaves. Add another layer of aubergine slices and repeat until you finish with tomato sauce. Drizzle a little oil on top and cook in the oven for half an hour. You can serve this dish hot, but it's also very good cold.

Beans

Beans form a large part of the Italian diet and there are over 400 varieties grown. In practice most Italians confine themselves to a few staples — the thin-skinned cannellini beans, the red spotted borlotti beans, runner beans and broad beans.

The biggest town in my Italian valley is Atina, and among its many claims to fame are its cannellini beans. In Italy, the most prized cannellini are the ones with the thinnest skins, and the ones from Atina are very thin skinned. The reason for this preference is simple – the thicker the skin, the more digestive gases are produced.

From June to autumn, beans can be bought fresh in the markets, but for the rest of the year they are dried. Dried beans can keep for years and they don't lose their nutritive properties. They only need to be rehydrated by soaking them in water and they're ready to cook.

In my part of Italy they make a terracotta jar with two handles on the same side that was traditionally used to cook beans. You filled the jar with water and beans and left it in front of the fire before you went to bed, the two handles facing away from the flames. By the next morning, the slow heat of the dying embers would have cooked the beans and you'd be able to touch the handles without burning your fingers.

You won't have the same choice of beans in Ireland as Italians do, but borlotti and cannellini can be found easily enough in tins. If you buy tins of beans, all you need to do is heat them up. If you can find dried beans, leave them to soak in water overnight before you cook them and discard any that float. They'll need 2 to 3 hours of cooking at a simmer. Test them for softness after 2 hours, and if they're still hard, keep cooking them.

In the unlikely event that you can find fresh beans, they cook in about an hour, but start testing them for softness after 40 minutes.

Fagioli alla Pizzaiola – BEANS IN A TOMATO SAUCE

If you're using dried beans, cook them with a little crushed garlic and a couple of sage leaves. If you're using tinned beans, simply heat them up along with the crushed garlic and sage. Make Paolo's tomato sauce as per the recipe on p. 38 and pour it over the beans, stirring carefully so as not to break up the beans.

Fagioli e Salsiccie – SAUSAGES AND BEANS

You can serve this as a first course in place of pasta. In my part of Italy it's used as a warming winter dish, nutritious and filling.

If you're using dried beans, cook them with a little crushed garlic and a couple of sage leaves. If you're using tinned beans, simply heat them up along with the crushed garlic and sage. While they're cooking, prick 4 Italian sausages (*salsiccie*) a few times with a fork and fry them in olive oil over a medium heat until they're browned all over. If you like, you can add a splash of red wine while the sausages are cooking and let it evaporate. When the sausages are cooked, cut them up into bite-sized pieces. Add the drained beans to the sausages, stirring them carefully so you don't break up the beans.

Fagioli in Puré – PURÉED BEANS

If you're using dried beans, cook them with a little crushed garlic and a couple of sage leaves. If you're using tinned beans, simply heat them up along with the crushed garlic and sage. Make up half a litre of vegetable stock. When the beans are cooked, use a stick blender to purée them, adding the stock a little at a time. You may not need all of it.

When the purée is at the desired consistency, season it with salt and freshly ground black pepper. This dish goes well with roasted meats.

Cauliflower

Cavolofiore al Gorgonzola – CAULIFLOWER CHEESE

This is cauliflower cheese with a difference, and the difference is Gorgonzola, one of Italy's best-known cheeses. If, like me, you find cauliflower just a bit dull, this might tempt you to eat it.

One kilo of cauliflower is enough for 4 people. Cook it in boiling salted water for about 15 minutes, until it's just tender. Remove it from the pot and put it in a serving bowl.

While it's cooking, put 250 grams of Gorgonzola, broken into pieces, in a blender with 100 ml of milk, 30 grams of butter and a splash of brandy. Liquidise it all together and pour this over the cauliflower.

Cabbage

I can't be the only one who was put off cabbage at an early age. I can still remember the cloying smell of cabbage that was boiled for hours on end until the whole place reeked of it.

Provincial hotels in Ireland had a particular smell, and the main element of the smell was boiled cabbage. Overcooking any member of the cabbage family releases a sulphurous smell. I've never found out why it was deemed necessary to cook it for so long. These days, I cook cabbage in a wide-bottomed casserole pot with a lid. Here's how.

Cavolo in Padella –
Pan-cooked Cabbage

Thinly slice half a Savoy cabbage and shake out the slices to free the strips. Put them in a pot and salt them, then pour a glass of white wine over them and put on the lid. Put the pot on a low heat and let it cook in its own juices, stirring from time to time. After about 15 minutes, the cabbage will be soft. Remove the lid and let the remaining liquid boil away, then serve.

I often make a variation of this by first browning bacon lardons in the pot before adding the cabbage, then proceed as above. You'll get that old-fashioned taste of bacon and cabbage, but the texture will still be firm.

Involtini di Cavolo alla Ricotta –
Cabbage Rolls with Ricotta

This is a bit of fun. Blanch 8 of the outer leaves from a Savoy cabbage in boiling salted water for 5 minutes. Take them out of the water, dip them in iced water and put them on a clean tea towel to drain. Now cook 300 grams of Swiss chard or Chinese leaf in the same water for 15 minutes.

Remove the chard and squeeze as much water out of it as you can. Chop it up and mix it in a bowl with 200 grams of ricotta,

100 grams of freshly grated Parmesan and 2 eggs. Season the mix and divide it among the 8 cabbage leaves, rolling each one up. Use kitchen string to tie the ends of each roll, or they will unravel.

Line your cabbage rolls up in a casserole dish and pour Paolo's tomato sauce (p. 38) over them. Put on the lid and let it simmer gently for 20 minutes before serving.

French Beans

Fagiolini al'Uova – FRENCH BEANS WITH EGG

This is one of those really simple dishes that creates a big effect. It makes an interesting side dish for main courses and it presents really well. It uses the same technique that's used when making a *carbonara* (p. 48).

Cook 500 grams of French beans in boiling salted water for about 15 minutes, then drain them and cut into bite-sized pieces.

While they're cooking, chop up 2 small onions and fry them in olive oil over a medium heat for 5 minutes. Whisk 2 eggs with 30 grams of freshly grated Parmesan and season with salt and freshly ground black pepper.

Add the chopped beans to the onions and stir them together, cooking for a few minutes, then pour the egg mixture in, stirring constantly, and remove the pan from the heat. The residual heat of the beans and onions will cook the egg and you should end up with a creamy sauce.

Lentils

Lentils are very common in Italian cookery, partly because they taste good and partly because they're both cheap and nutritious.

The best lentils in Italy come from Norcia in Umbria, which is also a centre of the truffle trade. Like dried beans, dried lentils need to be soaked in water for a few hours before cooking, but don't overdo it or they'll start to sprout. Just as with beans, if any float, discard them.

Lentils turn up frequently in soups, but they're also served alone as a side dish. They're very good simply prepared, with just a little olive oil, a dash of vinegar and some chopped basil leaves. Another good recipe is to serve them with Italian sausages – use the recipe for sausages and beans on pp. 103–4 and just replace the beans with lentils. They're often served in a tomato sauce, so make Paolo's tomato sauce as per the recipe on p. 38, then stir it into the cooked lentils before serving.

Lentils need to cook for about an hour and a half in simmering salted water. You can flavour the cooking water with a chopped onion and a celery stick.

Lenticchie al Bacon –
LENTILS WITH BACON

This simple dish works just as well with cannellini beans, so you can them instead of lentils.

Cook 300 grams of lentils for an hour and a half, then drain them and season them.

Cook 100 grams of bacon lardons in a pot with olive oil and a crushed clove of garlic until the fat starts to run. Add the lentils to the bacon and stir well, checking for seasoning before serving.

Mushrooms

The greatest gift of autumn is fungi. They appear at other times of the year, but the mushrooms that interest the gastronome are autumnal ones, the chanterelles and the ceps. In Italy, ceps are called porcini, and apart from truffles, they are regarded as the finest mushrooms.

They do grow in Ireland, where they are known as penny buns because the large brown cap looks like a well-cooked bun. They grow in symbiosis with trees, specifically oak and beech, so they're forest mushrooms, not field mushrooms.

They are wonderful when fresh, the flesh is firm and they have a glorious taste. To be honest, I've found that the porcini that grow here tend to have less intensity of flavour, perhaps because they get more rain and grow that much quicker. But even if you can't find fresh porcini, they're easily bought in their dried form.

Porcini are perfect for the larder. If you should be lucky enough to pick more than you can eat, you can dry the surplus by slicing them thinly and leaving them racked above a radiator. When needed, soak them in a little water for 20 minutes or so and they will reconstitute. A friend of mine in Italy dries his sliced ceps on a sprig of blackthorn that he sticks in a flowerpot. Each spike is home to a slice of cep and they dry well like this, as well as looking like a work of art.

A good idea for storing any dried mushrooms is to put them in a jar with little packets of desiccant, which you can find in the packaging of lots of different things. They're small packets designed to absorb moisture, so they're a great help in storing your mushrooms.

A large cep – I've found one weighing over 800 grams – can be sliced like a steak. Dip the slices in beaten egg and then breadcrumbs and fry till golden on both sides. The flesh stays firm and doesn't shrink, so this method of cooking works well. If you're fortunate enough to find a giant puffball before it has begun to spore, then you can cook it like this as well – a poor man's veal cutlet.

Porcini al Prosciutto – Ceps with Prosciutto

It's not surprising that Italians have thought of combining two of their favourite foods, and in fact, they do go very nicely together. Mushrooms have a curious property of absorbing salt and you always need more than you think, so salty prosciutto makes a good combination.

If you're using dried porcini, put them in a small bowl with enough water to cover them. They are hydrophilic, so will readily absorb the water and reconstitute. If there's any water left after they've reconstituted, don't throw it away – it will have plenty of mushroom taste in it. You may need to strain it though, as sometimes dried porcini come with a little earth or sand and you don't need that in your final dish.

Cook 500 grams of porcini over a medium heat for 5 minutes in olive oil, then add a glass of white wine and 150 grams of diced prosciutto. Let the wine evaporate, then add a clove of crushed garlic and a sprinkle of oregano. Cover the pan and let it all cook together for 20 minutes, stirring occasionally. Check the seasoning before serving.

Onions

There's almost no dish in which onions don't make an appearance — they're integral to much of Italian cookery. They don't often make a solo appearance, but *cipolle ripiene* is a dish where they do.

Cipolle Ripiene – Stuffed Onions

Preheat the oven to 180°C. You'll need 4 large onions, 1 per person. Parboil them in salted water for 5 minutes, then remove from the pot and set them aside to cool. Meanwhile, to prepare the stuffing, fry 150 grams of minced beef in olive oil over a medium heat and put 2 slices of bread without the crusts in a saucer of milk. When the mince is cooked, squeeze out the excess milk from the bread. Mix the mince in a bowl with the bread, 1 beaten egg, some freshly grated Parmesan and salt and freshly ground black pepper.

Cut the onions in half, across rather than down. Carefully remove the centres with a spoon, leaving the outside in one piece. Chop up the onion that you've removed and add it to the meat mixture, stirring it in well. Fill the onion halves with the mixture and top each one with a knob of butter.

Put the onions in an ovenproof dish and add 2 centimetres or so of water so that the bottoms of the onions are covered. Bake them for half an hour. Sprinkle a little freshly grated Parmesan on them before serving.

Peas

Italians eat peas in much the same way as other people do, but there is a way of cooking them that I've never seen anywhere else. I learned it many years ago from a cattle dealer called Guido Schiavi, who loved to cook.

Piselli alla Pancetta – Peas with Bacon

If you're starting with fresh peas, cook them in boiling salted water for about 15 minutes, or until they're tender, then drain. While they're cooking, fry 100 grams of diced pancetta or bacon lardons in olive oil over a medium heat until they're golden brown. Add the strained peas and stir well, cooking them together for another 5 minutes before serving.

If you're using frozen peas, you can make this dish with just one pot. Fry the pancetta or the lardons in olive oil in a saucepan over a medium heat, and as soon as the fat starts to run, pour 500 grams of frozen peas into the pan and stir. Put a lid on the pan and stir every few minutes. After about 15 minutes, start checking the peas for softness. They cook very well like this without adding any water.

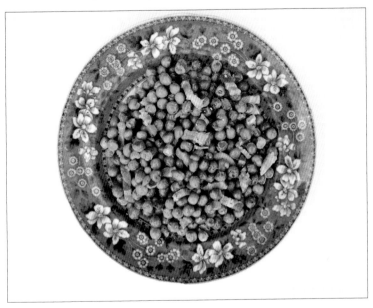

Peppers

Along with aubergines, sweet peppers are the quintessential Italian vegetable. In Italy, peppers are never eaten raw. There's a generally held belief that when raw they're indigestible for anyone over the age of 21. They're most commonly roasted until the skin is blackened, then the skin is removed along with the seeds and the flesh is ready for eating. Sweet peppers are called *peperoni* in Italian, so don't confuse that with the sausage in Ireland of the same name.

Peperoni Ripieni – STUFFED PEPPERS

Peppers are commonly served in strips flavoured with oil and garlic, as per the recipe on p. 26, or as a *peperonata* as per the recipe on p. 27. But they also work well stuffed, as in this recipe.

4 peppers

2 large or 3 medium potatoes, cut into small cubes

1 aubergine, cut into small cubes

2 large tomatoes, diced

2 or 3 chopped anchovy fillets

150 grams Emmental, diced

100 grams olives, chopped

1 teaspoon chopped capers

salt and freshly ground black pepper

olive oil

Preheat the oven to 180°C. Use a sharp knife to cut off the tops of the peppers, then using a knife and spoon, remove the hard membrane and the seeds from the insides, trying not to puncture the skin.

To make the stuffing, mix the potatoes, aubergines and diced tomatoes in a bowl with the anchovy fillets, diced cheese, olives, capers, salt and freshly ground black pepper and a drizzle of olive oil.

Fill the empty pepper shells with this mixture, drizzling a little oil into the top of each when filled. Replace the tops, put the peppers into an ovenproof dish and bake for about one hour.

Potatoes

Potatoes in Italian cooking come as they do in other cuisines — boiled, baked, fried, chipped and roasted. But there is one way of cooking potatoes that is particularly Italian, and it's how you often get them in restaurants.

Patate Saltate al Rosmarino – SAUTÉED POTATOES WITH GARLIC AND ROSEMARY

You'll need quite a lot of olive oil for this, so use a cheap oil, and after you've finished, strain it back into a bottle so that you can use it again.

Cook 500 grams of potatoes for 20 minutes in boiling salted water, then strain. Allow them to cool and cut them into 1-centimetre cubes.

Half fill a frying pan with oil and let it heat until it just begins to smoke. Carefully put your potato cubes into the oil, trying to avoid splashes of hot oil. Try to ensure that all the pieces are on one level in the pan. You can leave the potatoes frying in the oil for 20 minutes or much longer, depending on how crispy you want them to be. A few minutes before they're at the stage you like them, add some chopped rosemary and crushed garlic. Salt the potato cubes once you've removed them from the pan.

Sprouts

How many people do you know that eat sprouts other than on Christmas Day? Few, I'll bet. Children certainly seem to have a deep aversion to sprouts, yet there are ways of presenting sprouts that can transform them from a vegetable that few admire into a dish that will have people asking for more.

Cavoletti al'Aglio –
SPROUTS WITH BREADCRUMBS

The easiest way to spruce up a sprout is with garlic breadcrumbs. Crush a couple of cloves of garlic into a frying pan with olive oil and let the garlic cook for a few moments on a low heat, then add some breadcrumbs and stir. If the breadcrumbs quickly soak up all of the oil, add a little more until the breadcrumbs are browned and flavoured with garlic.

Meanwhile, cook the sprouts for 15 minutes in boiling salted water, drain them and toss them in the garlic breadcrumbs before serving.

Tomatoes

Whenever I get to Italy, one of the first things that I want to do is eat some tomatoes. I rarely get the same urge in Ireland, mainly because the tomatoes in the shops and supermarkets have almost no taste.

There's something about a sun-ripened tomato that sets my senses reeling – the smell, the taste and the visual beauty. When you take a dish like a Caprese salad, which only has four ingredients, if any one of those ingredients isn't the best, the whole dish fails.

I have been presented with Caprese salads in Ireland made from unripe greenhouse tomatoes, Danish mozzarella, dried basil and nasty olive oil. It couldn't have been further from what you'd get in Capri – buffalo mozzarella, sun-ripened San Marzano tomatoes, fresh basil leaves and extra virgin olive oil.

Insalata di Pomodori e Cipolle – TOMATO AND ONION SALAD

My friend Graziano Lucarelli has a vegetable garden at the back of his house and I love to visit him. We'll go to the tomato plants, pick a few and then an onion or two and bring them into the house. We chop them up haphazardly – that's to say we cut both the tomatoes and the onions a chunk at a time, changing the direction and the angle of the cut each time. It makes a change from regular slices.

We mix these in equal amounts, add some salt and then the olive oil made from Graziano's own olive trees. You may think I'm exaggerating when I say it's sublime, but it is. Okay, so you don't have access to Graziano's garden, but look for ripe beef tomatoes and well-formed onions, use good olive oil and you'll come very close.

Fagottini di Pomodori e Mozzarella –
TOMATO AND MOZZARELLA PARCELS

If you've ever eaten a Caprese salad, you'll know that tomatoes and mozzarella go well together. This recipe combines them with a theatrical touch of enclosing them in a parcel.

Preheat the oven to 200°C. Cut the tops off 8 small tomatoes and spoon out the insides without breaking the skins. Mix together 200 grams of diced mozzarella, a few leaves of chopped basil and some chopped parsley, a drizzle of olive oil and salt and freshly ground black pepper. Use this mixture to fill the tomatoes.

Now you'll need about 300 grams of puff pastry – I buy the frozen variety. Roll it out so that you can cut it into 8 squares. Separate an egg and beat the white and the yolk separately.

Assemble the dish by wrapping each tomato in a slice of pancetta or bacon and place it in the centre of a pastry square. Brush the edges of the pastry with the egg white and then pinch the corners together, enclosing the tomato. Brush the outside of the parcel with the egg yolk.

Place the tomatoes on a baking tray and cook them for about 20 minutes.

Fish

The Italian attitude to fish is very different from the Irish one. It's always amazed me that an island in the middle of the Atlantic Ocean can have so little interest in fish. Most islands around the world make their living from fishing and fish figures heavily in the diet. Perhaps the Irish indifference to fish is left over from the years when fish was seen only as a penance food. For most Irish people, a real feast has to include meat.

In Italy, if you want to honour a guest, you'll serve them fish – as a starter and as a main course. Apart from the fact that fish is seen as food for special occasions, it's also expensive. That seems fair enough to me – it's a dwindling resource and we really ought to expect to pay for it.

PAOLO TULLIO COOKS ITALIAN

Cod

When I was a child, my part of Italy was very much a rural backwater. There were still houses with no electricity and many of the houses that had it used it only for lighting. Fridges had yet to become a standard household item. Since we were a long way from the sea — the Comino Valley is almost exactly in the middle of the Italian peninsula — fresh fish wasn't a common sight.

What was common was the bright white, rock hard sides of salted air-dried cod, called *baccalà*. Because it was so hard, it had to be soaked in milk or water before you could use it. Every village had its own *Alimentari Generali*, or food shop, where the sides of *baccalà* would hang from the ceiling. You could buy a whole side, or the shopkeeper would cut off and weigh a piece to suit you. *Baccalà* was common all over the Mediterranean basin, from Portugal and Spain to southern France, Italy and the Balkan States.

It's not a taste that's much in fashion now, and in truth fresh fish is a far better food, but *baccalà* has had a long tradition and there are still many people who like its taste. It's not one of my favourite foods, but it's a part of my early life and so I'll include one dish with *baccalà* that I do like, which is called *brandade*. In French and English you don't pronounce the 'e', but in Italian you do.

Brandade

Soak 1 kilo of *baccalà* in water, changing the water three times, until it has softened. Remove it from the water, and if there are any pieces of bone or skin, remove them. Cut it into small pieces and poach it in water for about 10 minutes.

Cover the bottom of a pan with olive oil and let it heat until it smokes. Reduce the heat to low, add the cod and begin to work it into a purée with a wooden spoon, keeping it on a low heat. When it has formed a fine paste, add enough olive oil and cream to reach the desired consistency, stirring all the time. It should end up the consistency of puréed potatoes. Season it with salt and freshly ground black pepper. You can serve it garnished with croutons, or you can put it in an ovenproof dish and brown the top under a grill before serving.

Crab

This is a dish I used to serve in my restaurant many years ago. It was always a success, but I've never seen it since. It's one of those dishes that's easy to do but looks great. You get a lot of kudos for the effort you put in.

Fagottini di Granchio – Crab Puffs

I've spent many hours taking the flesh from freshly cooked crabs, but these days I do it the easy way and buy the crab meat. You'll need about 200 grams for 4 people.

Preheat the oven to 200°C. Squeeze as much liquid as you can from the crab meat and mix it together with enough garlic mayonnaise to moisten the crab meat well. You can buy garlic mayonnaise or make it as per the recipe on pp. 18–19.

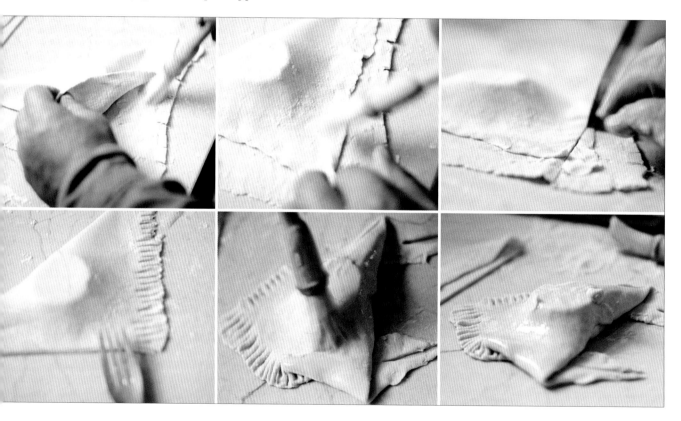

Roll out 200 grams of puff pastry so that you can cut it into 4 squares, as accurately as you can. Divide the crab meat between the 4 squares, placing it in the middle. Beat an egg and brush it onto 2 sides of each square. Fold each square across the diagonal, making a triangle. Seal all around the edges with the back of a fork.

Turn each puff so that the long side is facing you. Turn the two corners facing you underneath the puff and the corner at the back upwards. Make 2 small balls of pastry and place them as the crab's eyes, sticking them on with some of the beaten egg. Brush the puffs with the remaining beaten egg and cook them in the oven for 15 minutes.

John Dory

John Dory is another common Mediterranean fish. In Italian it's called St Peter's fish, because legend has it that he picked one up between his thumb and forefinger and left a spot on either side of the fish's flanks.

Involtini di San Pietro – ROULADES OF JOHN DORY

This recipe was one my Aunt Giulia used to make when we went to visit her, as she knew it was one of my favourites.

You'll need 1 tin of anchovy fillets, garlic, some breadcrumbs, Parmesan, parsley, thyme, rosemary and lemon, as well as about 500 grams of John Dory fillets.

Preheat the oven to 180°C. Chop up the anchovies and mix them in a bowl with a crushed clove of garlic, 60 grams of breadcrumbs, about 60 grams of freshly grated Parmesan, the herbs and a little olive oil to bind it all together. Season with salt and freshly ground black pepper. Divide this among the fish fillets, rolling them up and fixing them with a cocktail stick. Put them in an ovenproof dish and sprinkle them with chopped rosemary and a little lemon juice. Cook them in the oven for 15 minutes.

Mackerel

Mackerel is much more highly prized in Italy than it is in Ireland, possibly because it's less commonplace. It's one of my favourite fish, and according to many nutritionists, its oily flesh is full of those magic omega-3 oils that keep the grey cells functioning. This is a very simple recipe, but it's tasty and might convert those who are still unsure about mackerel.

Sgombro al Burro – MACKEREL WITH SAGE BUTTER

Allowing 1 fish per person, make a few diagonal cuts in the flesh on both sides of the fish. Fry them in butter over a medium heat for about 5 minutes on each side. Season them and set them aside.

Make a little sage butter by melting 100 grams of butter in a small pot with a dozen sage leaves. When the leaves have become crisp, remove the pot from the heat. Pour a little of this sage butter on each mackerel, adding a dash of lemon juice.

Mussels

I've loved mussels for as long as I can remember. I can also remember wishing that one day I'd be able to say, 'Thank you, I've had enough mussels.' Some years later, I was saying this to my friend Gay Brabazon when I was staying at her house on Clew Bay. She instructed me to get a couple of fertilizer sacks and drove me to Killary Harbour, where we collected sackfuls of mussels before returning home. We had a huge saucepan, but even so it took four separate boilings to cook all the mussels. Then we sat down and shelled them all until all we had was a big pile of mussel meat. We ate some with garlic butter, some with a Provençal sauce and some plain. Eventually I was able to say, 'Thank you, I've had enough.'

Cozze con Pepperoni — Mussels with Peppers

Here's how I ate mussels in Naples once. Put 1 kilo of mussels in a pot with a clove of garlic and some olive oil over a high heat for about 5 minutes, when they should have all opened. Discard any that remain closed. Shell the mussels and put them aside.

Slice up 2 green peppers and make sure you've removed all the seeds. Cook the slices in a pan with olive oil and a clove of garlic over a medium heat, stirring often. They should be cooked in about 10 minutes. Stir in the mussels, season them and add some chopped thyme before serving.

Octopus

Octopus is highly prized in Italy, but it needs to be treated carefully or it can be tough. The most tender octopus are the very small young males. Apart from the eyes and the beak, the entire animal is edible.

Larger octopus need to be tenderised immediately after they're caught. You'll often see fishermen bashing an octopus on the harbour wall over and over again in order to tenderise the flesh.

Insalata di Polpo – Octopus Salad

For this salad you'll need an octopus weighing about 1 kilo, or the same weight of smaller ones. Cook the octopus in a large pan covered in water with a pinch of salt. Bring the water to the boil, then turn down the heat to a simmer. Cook the octopus for about half an hour, or a little longer if it's still not tender. Let it cool down in the water, then drain it, skin it and cut it into small pieces.

Meanwhile, boil 5 or 6 potatoes in salted water for 25 minutes, or until they're tender, then drain them, peel them and dice them into 1-centimetre cubes.

Mix the octopus and potatoes together in a serving bowl, adding a little olive oil and a splash of white wine. Check the seasoning and sprinkle with chopped rosemary.

Sea Bass

Nearly all the sea bass sold in Ireland these days is farmed. Line-caught wild sea bass can be found now and then, and occasionally some come in from France. Most of the time, though, you'll be buying farmed fillets. Cooking them in parchment paper like this is a good way of injecting flavour into farmed fish.

Brandino in Cartoccio –
SEA BASS IN A PARCEL

A 1-kilo fish will feed 4 people, otherwise use 1 fillet per person.

Preheat the oven to 200°C. Cut a sheet of baking parchment paper, oil it well and place the fish in the centre of it. Or wrap fillets two at a time, flesh side to flesh side. Put a sprig of rosemary and a clove of garlic into the cavity of the fish and season with salt and freshly ground black pepper. Sprinkle some chopped parsley on the fish and cover the sides with sliced lemon. Splash about half a glass of white wine over the fish and wrap it up in the parchment, taking care to seal the edges as tightly as you can.

Put it in the oven for between 12 and 15 minutes. Serve with a drizzle of olive oil and a piece of lemon.

Squid

Perhaps squid are best known when cut into rings, battered and fried, when they go by their Italian name of *calamari*. Good as they are like that, they're delicious prepared in a variety of ways.

To prepare squid, pull the head and tentacles from the body sac. Squeeze the sac and pull the translucent quill out. Rub your fingers over the body sac under running water and remove the skin. Cut the head away from the tentacles and discard, keeping the tentacles.

As a rule, it's better to buy small squid, which are more tender and more versatile. Big ones are best cut into rings. Many Italians keep the ink from the ink sac and use it to colour and flavour pasta.

Calamari Ripieni – STUFFED SQUID

Clean 4 squid. Chop up the tentacles and mix with a crushed clove of garlic, some breadcrumbs and olive oil to make the stuffing. Spoon this mixture into the body cavities of the squid and close the open end with a cocktail stick. Brush the squid with olive oil and season them with salt and freshly ground black pepper. Grill them, turning them often until they're golden and tender. Serve them with lemon wedges.

Calamari alla Griglia – GRILLED SQUID

Clean 4 squid and slice the body sac open to make 2 pieces. Make sure it's properly cleaned, then take a sharp knife and score the flesh on the inside in parallel diagonal lines, then again at 90 degrees to the first cuts, making a diamond pattern.

Cook the *calamari*, scored side down first, in a heavy skillet or griddle, then turn them over. They should open out, revealing the diamond shapes that you cut. Season them and serve them with a few drops of chilli oil as per the recipe on p. 178, or just break up a chilli into a ramekin of oil and use drops of this for flavouring.

Swordfish

The nearest beach to my Italian house is between Formia and Gaeta on the Tyrrhenian Coast. It's a busy coastline, full of holiday homes belonging to Romans and Neapolitans, as it's almost halfway between these two cities. All along the lidos are restaurants specialising in fish, and it's here we come when we want a fish feast.

Pesce Spada all'Aceto Balsamico — SWORDFISH WITH BALSAMIC VINEGAR

No fish is more typical of the Mediterranean than the swordfish. It has a firm, meaty flesh and in the fish markets you can often find monsters 2.5 metres long, laid out on a slab. The fishmonger will cut steaks from it to order. This recipe combines this fish with another flavour that's very typical of Italy – balsamic vinegar.

Put 4 swordfish steaks into a bowl and cover them with milk. Let them stand for about 15 minutes, then drain them and dust them with flour. Heat 100 grams of butter in a pan over a medium heat and brown the steaks until they're golden on both sides. Season them and set them aside, keeping them warm.

Melt 100 grams of butter in a pot and add 1 flat teaspoon of ground cinnamon, 1 whole clove and 100 ml of balsamic vinegar. Let it simmer until it thickens, stirring occasionally. Pour this sauce over the fish before serving.

Trout

This is a recipe I learned from the chef in one of my region's great restaurants, Mantova sul Lago. It's in the most beautiful setting, on the banks of the River Fibreno overlooking the lake of the same name. I ate there often as a boy with my parents and I still go — for the food, but also for the amazing views.

Trotta con Pancetta —
TROUT WITH PANCETTA

Pancetta is a mildly cured cut of pork belly that is very similar to streaky bacon, which we use if no pancetta is to hand.

Preheat the oven to 180°C. Either fillet fresh trout or buy the pre-prepared fillets. Slice each fillet in half lengthways and remove any remaining bones using kitchen tweezers. Trim a slice of streaky bacon to the size of the fillet and plait the bacon and fillet together. An elegant tying technique is to blanch an outer leaf of a leek or an onion leaf for a couple of minutes in boiling water. You can then tear thin strips off along the length, which you can use to tie the ends of the plaits together so that they won't unravel.

Heat a frying pan with a little olive oil over a medium heat, and when it's hot, place the tied fillets gently in the pan. Turn after 1 minute and allow 1 minute for the other side. Place the fillets on a baking tray, pour a little melted butter over them and put them in the oven for 5 minutes or so. Serve this dish with its own pan juices and a little freshly ground pepper and accompany it with a rocket salad.

Veal

Veal is common in Italy because it's tender, unlike the beef. It can be cooked more easily — for example, it can be simply fried. Veal is available in Ireland, but its means of production puts a lot of people off, and since our beef is tender, there's no real reason to use it. I frequently substitute pork fillet or pork steak for veal. The colour is right, the texture is similar and once cooked, the taste is virtually indistinguishable.

Wherever I've called for veal in a recipe, you can use pork fillet cut this way instead. One pork fillet will serve four. First trim the fillet well, removing any fatty bits and membrane that are still on it. I cut big fillets into four, smaller ones into three. Take each piece, one at a time, and hold it firmly to a chopping board with the hand that you don't use for cutting pressing down hard. Now take a sharp knife and make a parallel cut as close as you can to the board. Don't complete the cut when you get to the other end, but rather pull the thick part – the top part – over and continue cutting. Imagine that you're opening up a Swiss roll with your knife. The thinner you can cut it, the better.

If you're careful, you can end up with a dozen or so pieces that are about 8 centimetres by 5 centimetres. Don't worry if you can't get the pieces the same size, just try to keep them thin.

Saltimbocca alla Romana – Roman 'Jump in the Mouth'

This is a real classic from Rome. Cover the bottom of a heavy-bottomed skillet or frying pan with olive oil. Dust each piece of thinly cut veal in seasoned flour – that's flour with salt and freshly ground black pepper added. Cut a slice of prosciutto to fit on top of the veal, then place a large sage leaf between the pork and the prosciutto. Now pin the three elements together with a cocktail stick.

Occasionally you'll find them in Italy presented rolled up, with the cocktail stick serving to keep it from unrolling, but traditionally it's kept flat. As your little packets cook in the frying pan, add a glass of white wine and let it boil off. The flour will thicken the cooking juices, which become the sauce that you serve it with. Garnish the plate with a piece of lemon.

Escalopes alla Milanese – Veal Milanese

This is a dish I love to make using pork fillet. Most recipes will tell you to dip each slice of meat into flour, then beaten egg, then breadcrumbs. Do that if you like, but I prefer to make a *panada*, which is made with flour and water. Put some flour into a soup bowl, add some salt and freshly ground black pepper, then add water while you mix it with a fork. Add enough water for the *panada* to be thick like cream. Dip the pieces of meat into this, and then into the breadcrumbs.

Shallow fry the pieces in batches in olive oil over a medium heat, keeping the cooked pieces warm while you cook the rest. I love these even when they're cold the next day, so I always make more than I know we're going to eat.

This is a simple way to make meat go a long way, so garnish it with a slice of lemon and serve it with something simple like *risotto alla Milanese* (p. 75) or even just a green salad.

Involtini alle Verdure – Veal Roulades

Involtini, or roulades, are a common way of serving thin slices of veal. It gives you the opportunity to include different tastes into your veal slice. This recipe is quite common, but you can use exactly the same method with the filling of your choice.

Cut 2 carrots and 1 celery stick into batons and divide them between the veal slices. Roll up the slices and pin them together with a cocktail stick, pinning them so that the stick is almost flush with the sides, so that you'll be able to turn them in the pan. Brown them in a pan, season them and add half a glass of white wine. Let the wine boil off, then add 4 tablespoons of passata. Put a lid on the pan and let it simmer gently for half an hour before serving.

Beef

Bistecca alla Pizzaiola – Steak with a *Pizzaiola* Sauce

This dish was developed around the Naples region to deal with their proverbially tough meat. There's no point in doing this with meat that's already tender, like fillet, sirloin or strip loin. Use a cheaper cut like round steak and ask your butcher to slice it thinly for you – about half a centimetre thick.

First make the *pizzaiola* sauce as described on p. 36. Brown the steaks in a pan with olive oil over a medium heat and a little crushed garlic for about 1 minute on each side. When they're brown on both sides, season with salt and freshly ground black pepper and cover the steaks with the *pizzaiola* sauce.

Put a lid on the pan, turn the heat down and leave them to cook for a further 5 to 8 minutes, depending on how well you like your steaks cooked.

Serve the steaks in their sauce and top them off with chopped basil or oregano, though parsley will do at a pinch.

Ossobuco

You'll need a friendly butcher to make this dish, as it's a cut Irish butchers don't usually do. What you need are steaks about 2.5 centimetres thick cut across the beef shinbone. You end up with a round of meat with a circular section of shinbone right in the middle. That's what gives this dish its name, which means 'bone with a hole'.

for the ossobuco:
4 steaks, cut across the shinbone
seasoned flour
butter
olive oil
4 beef tomatoes, sliced into rounds
3 sticks of celery, grated
3 cloves of garlic, crushed
2 onions, chopped
1 glass of wine
250 ml stock
bay leaves

for the gremolata:
2 large cloves of garlic
rind of 2 medium lemons
an equal measure of fresh parsley

Because you're going to use a cheaper cut of meat, you're going to use a long and slow cooking process. First coat your meat with seasoned flour and then brown the pieces on both sides in a frying pan over a medium heat with a little butter and olive oil. When they're browned, remove them from the pan and set them aside.

Put the tomatoes, celery, garlic and onions into the pan and let the vegetables start to soften over a low heat for about 15 minutes. Place your pieces of browned meat on top of the vegetable base and add the wine, stock and a couple of bay leaves. Put a lid on the pan and let it simmer on a low heat for an hour and a half, turning the meat a couple of times while it cooks.

Meanwhile, prepare the *gremolata*, which is the classic accompaniment for *ossobuco*. You make it with one part garlic, one part lemon zest and one part parsley. Put the garlic through a crusher, zest the lemon and chop the parsley, then combine them into your *gremolata*.

When you're ready to serve, remove the meat from the pan and set it aside. Now quickly blend the vegetables in the pan either with a stick blender or push then through a coarse sieve. Use this as your sauce to cover the meat and sprinkle the *gremolata* on top.

I like to serve *ossobuco* with rice or mashed potato.

Lesso al Rosmarino –
POACHED BEEF WITH ROSEMARY

Poached meat is fairly common in Italy, because it makes tough meat tender. This is a very easy and tasty recipe that my grandmother used to make. As ever, use thin slices of beef. Rib or round steak works very well. Keep it simple and serve with boiled potatoes.

Start by browning your steaks quickly in a pan with olive oil over a medium heat for about 1 minute on each side, then season them. Chop a sprig of rosemary and a clove of garlic and mix them together with a good splash of white wine vinegar. Turn the heat down in the pan, cover the steaks with the vinegar mixture and put a lid on the pan. This will keep in the steam and help the beef poach, the vinegar will help break down the fibres in the meat and the rosemary will perfume the dish.

Polpette

Polpette are meatballs and they're usually made from minced beef and minced pork. They turn up quite a lot in the Italian kitchen for two reasons – firstly, minced beef is tender, and secondly, making meatballs allows you to use up your stale bread, which you turn into breadcrumbs and add to the mince.

It's curious that the Italian dish that's so well known in America – spaghetti with meatballs – is entirely unknown in Italy. What seems to have happened is that early Italian immigrants working in New York would get their lunch packs from their wives. The wives would of course make their men pasta for lunch, and then give them meat for their second course. To make a neat package, they'd put the meatballs on top of the pasta. What the onlooking Americans saw was a single dish, while what the Italians saw was a plate of pasta with the second course sitting on top.

Polpette alla Casalinga –
HOUSEWIFE'S MEATBALLS

2 slices of white bread, broken up
milk
450 grams minced beef
110 grams sausage meat
2 or 3 cloves of garlic, crushed
1 egg, beaten
olive oil
salt and freshly ground black pepper

Soak the 2 slices of broken-up white bread in milk for 5 minutes, and then give it a light squeeze. Now put the bread, minced beef, sausage meat, garlic and beaten egg into a mixing bowl along with a splash of olive oil. Season it with salt and freshly ground black

pepper. Mix it all together well and roll the mixture into balls about the size of ping-pong balls. Place them on a tray and then put them in the fridge for 1 hour. This will stop them falling apart when you cook them.

Shallow fry them in olive oil over a medium heat for about 10 minutes, or until they're cooked through. Meanwhile, warm up some Paolo's tomato sauce as per the recipe on p. 38. Cover the meatballs with the sauce before serving.

Polpette con Spinace — MEATBALLS WITH SPINACH

This is a variation of the simple meatball recipe above and uses béchamel sauce, which acts as a binding agent. Make some béchamel using the recipe on p. 15 before you begin.

250 grams spinach

250 grams minced beef

30 grams freshly grated Parmesan

120 ml béchamel

1 egg, beaten

salt and freshly ground black pepper

plain flour

30 grams butter

olive oil

Start by cooking the spinach in a covered pot for about 5 minutes, when it will have wilted. There's no need to add any water, it will cook perfectly well with just the water that's left on it after washing. Drain it and squeeze out as much of the remaining liquid as you can and chop it finely.

Put the spinach, beef, Parmesan, béchamel and egg in a bowl and mix it well, seasoning it with salt and freshly ground black pepper. Make 8 balls from your meat mixture and roll each ball in plain flour before shallow frying them over a medium heat in the butter and oil. Turn them frequently until they're browned all over and serve.

Tartara di Manzo — STEAK TARTARE

Since my father introduced me to steak tartare as a boy, I've loved it. I do appreciate that you need to be a carnivore to enjoy it, but if you like rare beef, it's a small step to steak tartare. Personally, I like to mix it myself in restaurants, rather than have it brought to the table ready mixed. It's a good way to tenderise Italian beef.

You'll need 125 grams of beef per person, and traditionally it should be beef fillet. Ask your butcher to mince it twice. You may well get some funny looks, as to many butchers the idea of mincing fillet is crazy. I have used aged sirloin on occasion and it works very well.

You'll also need 1 really good egg per person, and by that I mean ideally a fresh farmyard egg, but if that's unavailable an organic, free-range egg will do.

Mix the minced beef with some olive oil, salt and freshly ground black pepper and shape each portion into a mound. Flatten this and make a dip in the middle. Put the raw egg yolk into this shallow well.

Surround the meat on the plate with little piles of finely chopped onion, chopped capers, chopped anchovies and chopped parsley plus a small dollop of mustard and a wedge of lemon.

Serving it like this allows each diner to mix the steak with exactly the quantities of the trimmings that suits them best.

Carpaccio

Carpaccio is becoming as common outside of Italy as it is in Italy. Like steak tartare, it's raw beef, but sliced wafer thin. And like steak tartare there's no actual cooking involved, just the preparation. This dish was invented by the famous chef Arrigo Cipriani, who served it in his renowned Venetian restaurant.

You will need mayonnaise for this dish and I urge you to make it yourself, rather than use a bought concoction. I'm not against bought mayonnaise, but since this dish contains only beef and mayonnaise, use the best beef you can find and use homemade mayonnaise. You can find the recipe on p. 18.

Spice the mayonnaise up a bit with 1 tablespoon of Worcestershire sauce and 1 tablespoon of lemon juice, then add 3 tablespoons of milk to thin it down. Finish it with a sprinkle of salt and freshly ground black pepper.

To serve 4 people, you'll need 500 grams of sirloin steak sliced wafer thin. Your butcher should be able to do this for you if you don't have a meat slice at home. Lay the thin slices of beef carefully on a serving platter and drizzle the mayonnaise mixture over it.

There are other versions without mayonnaise. You can simply drizzle the seasoned meat with olive oil and lemon juice, then cover it with shavings of Parmesan or even truffles.

Lamb

Lamb in Italy is always very young lamb, killed at around 20 kilos, which is half the weight they're killed at in Ireland. Because it's young and tender, it's normally cooked simply and quickly. It's the most commonly used meat on barbecues.

Costolette Scottadito – 'BURN YOUR FINGERS' LAMB CHOPS

Using 2 chops per person, brush them with olive oil and season them with salt and freshly ground black pepper. Put them somewhere cool for half an hour, then either put them under a hot grill or onto a hot pan, cooking them for 3 minutes on each side. Check the seasoning, squeeze lemon juice onto them and serve.

Costolette alla Brace – BARBECUE CHOPS

As before, brush the chops with olive oil and season them with salt and freshly ground black pepper. Make a brush from a few sprigs of rosemary tied together. Use the rosemary brush dipped into olive oil to baste the chops while they cook. When you've finished with it as a brush, put it in the embers and let its smoke perfume the chops.

Costolette al Burro d'Acciuga – LAMB CHOPS WITH ANCHOVY BUTTER

First you'll need to make the anchovy butter. Drain anchovy fillets from a tin well, drying them if necessary with kitchen paper, and chop them finely. Beat 100 grams of softened butter in a bowl until creamy, then add in the chopped anchovies and mix well. Anchovy butter goes well with many meats, but it's delicious on lamb.

Cook 2 lamb chops per person either under a grill or in a pan for around 5 minutes a side, depending on how well you like them cooked. Season them with salt and freshly ground black pepper and serve them with a dab of anchovy butter on top.

Pork

I've already mentioned that pork fillets, also know as pork steaks, can be a useful substitution for veal when opened out, but there's another way to prepare them which is much easier, and that's to cut them into medallions. That means you cut across the fillet to create small rounds about half a centimetre thick. Cut like this, the meat cooks quickly, so you have to be careful not to overcook it, as it will toughen.

H ere are two recipes that were firm favourites from the menu in my restaurant. Both are very simple and very tasty. One pork steak will feed four.

Medaglioni con Limone e Cumino –
PORK MEDALLIONS WITH LEMON AND CUMIN

Melt some butter in a frying pan, and keeping the heat low, place your medallions in the pan. Turn them after 1 minute and sprinkle ground cumin and salt on the cooked side. After another minute, turn the medallions again and squeeze the juice of a lemon around them. Sprinkle more ground cumin and salt on top. After another minute or so, take them off the heat and serve.

Medaglioni con Susine e Cardomomo –
PORK MEDALLIONS WITH CARDAMOM AND PLUMS

Melt some butter in a frying pan, and keeping the heat low, place your medallions in the pan. Turn them after 1 minute and sprinkle salt, freshly ground black pepper and ground cardamom on the cooked side. After another minute, turn the medallions again and sprinkle them with salt, pepper and cardamom. Remove the medallions from the pan and set aside. Now pour 120 ml of cream into the pan with 4 plums, sliced thinly. Let the cream and plums reduce until the cream has become the colour of straw, then add the medallions, turning them quickly in the sauce before serving.

Rabbit

When I was a child, every house that I visited in the Comino Valley had a back yard full of hens and rabbits. Wild rabbits are virtually unknown in Italy, largely because there are so many licensed hunters. However, rabbits raised in hutches are still common, although the battery variety is increasingly filling the supermarket shelves.

Wild Rabbit

Farmed rabbit can be treated like any white meat, but wild rabbit needs some special attention. Firstly, it will have a stronger flavour than the farmed variety, and secondly, its meat will be considerably tougher.

I deal with wild rabbit like this now: first piece the rabbit and then put them in a pot covered with water. Bring it to the boil, then throw away the water. Add fresh water, a chopped onion, some peppercorns and a few bay leaves. Bring this to the boil, then turn down the heat and leave it to simmer for between an hour and a half and 2 hours. Remove the rabbit pieces from the pot and let them stand for a while to dry off.

Meanwhile, heat a large pan with olive oil over a medium heat. Add the rabbit pieces after tossing them in seasoned flour, turning them frequently until they're browned all over. Add some crushed garlic and chopped rosemary and cook for another 5 minutes. Transfer the pieces to a serving dish.

Coniglio al Forno – ROAST RABBIT

If you like roast rabbit, then this is a dish that you'll need farmed rabbit for. Wild rabbit is simply too tough to be treated like this.

Preheat the oven to 180°C. Heat some olive oil in a casserole dish with a sprig of rosemary and a couple of crushed garlic cloves. Fry the rabbit pieces in this flavoured oil over a medium heat until browned all over. Season with salt and freshly ground black pepper, then put the casserole dish in the oven, turning the pieces from time to time, for 1 hour.

Chicken

When I'm in Italy, I'm lucky enough to be in a valley where traditional agriculture is still practised. That means I can get real hens, the ones that peck about outside eating bits of grain and grubs. You can always tell if a bird has really been free range by looking at the legs. Birds that have lived outdoors have long, thin legs – exactly the opposite of the short, fat legs of the battery bird. Drumsticks that are six or seven inches long are what to look for, as well as a yellow tinge to the skin.

Outside of rural areas like mine, battery birds are what are on sale. They have less taste, so they need some added when they're cooked. Chicken breasts work well as *involtini*, or roulades.

Involtini di Pollo alla Salvia – CHICKEN ROULADES WITH SAGE

Slice 4 chicken fillets as thinly as you can, then pound them with a meat mallet to flatten them further. Put 2 sage leaves on each piece and season with salt and freshly ground black pepper. Slice 100 grams of pancetta as thinly as you can. Now roll up each piece with the sage leaves inside, then wrap the pancetta around the outside. Use cocktail sticks to hold the roulades together. Brown them in a pan in olive oil over a medium heat, until they're browned all over, then add a splash of water or stock and put a lid on. Leave it on a low heat for 20 minutes, then serve.

Involtini di Pollo alle Acciughe e Capperi – CHICKEN ROULADES WITH CAPERS AND ANCHOVIES

Slice 4 chicken fillets as thinly as you can, then pound them with a meat mallet to flatten them further. Place 1 anchovy fillet, a few capers and a sliver of butter on each piece and roll it up, pinning it together with a cocktail stick.

Dust each roulade with flour and fry them in olive oil over a medium heat until they're brown all over. Add half a glass of wine, cover and leave on a low heat for 20 minutes. Just before serving, remove the lid and let the remaining wine evaporate.

Pollo alla Cacciatore – HUNTER'S CHICKEN

This is a real classic, known the length and breadth of Italy. There are a few regional variations – you can find it with mushrooms and with other vegetables – but this is the traditional recipe, and it works well even with an old bird.

First piece the chicken, then brown it all over in a casserole dish in olive oil over a medium heat. Add a chopped onion, a chopped carrot, a chopped stick of celery, a tin of chopped tomatoes and a glass of water or stock. Cover the pot and let it simmer for 45 minutes.

Before serving, check the seasoning and sprinkle with chopped parsley.

Offal

One of the main principles of provincial Italian cookery is that nothing is wasted. For example, there is no part of the pig that doesn't get eaten – even the bones and skin are used to flavour soups and stews. We lose a whole world of tastes when we insist on eating only the fillet of an animal and only the breast of a chicken. Offal may be cheap, and that might lead you to suppose that it's not good to eat, but in fact offal can be a gourmet delight. Sweetbreads are my favourite, so let's start with them.

Although all mammals have sweetbreads, only two kinds commonly come to the table – veal and sheep. Veal sweetbreads are considerably larger, but they have the small irritation that you need to remove their covering membrane. Sheep sweetbreads also have covering membranes, but they're much thinner and hardly noticeable when you eat them, so I don't usually bother removing them.

Animelle Impanate –
Sweetbreads in Breadcrumbs

This is one of the best ways to enjoy the taste of sweetbreads. You'll need 500 grams of sweetbreads, either calf or sheep. If you're using calves' sweetbreads, boil them for about 5 minutes, drain them and leave them to cool down. Carefully remove the covering membrane, which is like a sausage skin. Try not to break the sweetbreads as you do this.

Beat an egg in a bowl and have some breadcrumbs ready in another. Dip the sweetbreads in the egg, then into the breadcrumbs. Fry them in butter over a medium heat, turning them until they have a golden colour. Drain them on kitchen paper and serve them on a bed of a plain risotto.

If you're using sheep sweetbreads, put them into a pot covered with cold water and bring them to the boil. As soon as the water boils, take them off the heat and let them cool down. If you have the patience, you can skin them, but I never do. Proceed as above, dipping them first into beaten egg and then into the breadcrumbs before frying them.

Animelle al Vino Bianco — SWEETBREADS IN WHITE WINE

Sweetbreads are often cooked in butter, as it seems to bring out their flavour, and that's how we'll cook them in this recipe. Start by parboiling them for 5 minutes and letting them cool. Skin them and cut them into thin slices. Melt 50 grams of butter in a pan and add 1 clove of sliced garlic. As soon as the garlic browns, remove it from the pan. Now dust the slices of sweetbreads in flour and fry them in the pan over a medium heat until the slices are golden brown on both sides. Add a large glass of white wine and put the heat up until the wine has evaporated. Serve the sweetbreads with a sprig of parsley.

Stracotto di Coda di Manzo — OXTAIL STEW

Strictly speaking, oxtail isn't offal, but for many people it has the same odour of repugnance. I suspect that many of those who claim to dislike it may not ever have actually eaten it, since it is truly delicious.

Many people are put off it too because it's perceived as being difficult to cook, but here's a recipe that's blindingly simple and makes a really delicious meal. I learned this way of cooking it from my friend Ida Delicata in Italy, a truly wonderful cook. It's a recipe that breaks well-established rules, yet produces great results.

Get your butcher to piece 2 oxtails. You'll have about a dozen pieces from each oxtail, ranging from quite large ones to small pieces the size of a little finger from the tail's tip.

Using a heavy pot with a lid that will hold all the pieces with a bit of room to spare, fit the pieces into the pot as closely packed as you can, using the small pieces to fill gaps between larger pieces. Make up some beef stock using 2 stock cubes, enough to cover all the pieces with a little extra on top.

Put the pot on to boil, and as soon as it reaches the boil, turn down the heat to a gentle simmer. Leave it with the lid on for 3 hours, then remove the lid and let it cook for another hour. The liquid will reduce and thicken, and as it does you can turn the oxtail pieces, browning them in the liquid. That's it – that's all you have to do.

Serve them on a bed of mashed potato with some of the cooking juices in a bowl. I promise you, the recipients will ask for seconds.

Lingua di Manzo — Tongue

A lot of Irish people have been put off tongue because as a child it was served to them looking exactly like a big tongue and they were invited to eat slices of it. Yet tongue is probably the most tender part of the animal. If you instead cook it like this, you'll make converts.

Some years ago I had cut a tongue into cubes and was tossing them in tomato sauce when my daughter Isabella came to visit. She asked what I was cooking, and I said beef. She asked if she could have some and we sat down and ate a bowlful each, with Isabella saying what wonderfully tender beef it was. She loved it and when we'd finished she asked what cut of beef it was. When I said tongue, she gagged. 'Oh my god, Dad, why didn't you tell me? That's disgusting.'

I find her reaction both curious and commonplace. If you try this recipe, just tell people it's beef.

Put an ox tongue on to boil with a few bay leaves and some black peppercorns in the water. Bring it up to the boil, put a lid on the pot and turn the heat down to a gentle simmer. Let it cook for three and a half hours. Remove the tongue and let it cool, then with a sharp knife remove the skin and trim off any fatty bits.

Cut the trimmed meat into 1-centimetre cubes and toss them in Paolo's tomato sauce (p. 38). Serve it on a bed of mashed potatoes or *risotto Milanese* (p. 75).

Liver

Liver is one of those foods that many people remember from their childhood with horror. Certainly I can remember eating liver that was cooked for so long it had a texture like the sole of a shoe. Yet I know no one who doesn't like pâté, which is made from liver. Most people seem to like the taste, but not the texture.

The trick with cooking liver is not to overcook it. It toughens as it cooks, so be very careful not to keep it on the heat for too long.

Fegato alla Salvia – Liver with Sage

Slice 500 grams of calves' or lambs' liver. Beat 2 eggs with a little salt in a dish and place the slices of liver in the egg. Melt 60 grams of butter in a frying pan and add 6 sage leaves and 1 clove of crushed garlic. When the garlic is brown, remove it and the sage from the pan, which will leave the butter nicely flavoured. Take the liver from the egg and fry it in the butter over a medium heat for 1 minute on each side, then turn down the heat and let it cook for another 3 minutes at most, turning frequently. Season with salt and freshly ground black pepper before serving.

Fegato al Limone – Liver with Lemon

Slice 500 grams of calves' or lambs' liver and dip each piece into flour seasoned with salt and freshly ground black pepper. Melt 30 grams of butter with 2 tablespoons of olive oil in a pan, add the liver and turn up the heat. Turn the pieces frequently for 4 or 5 minutes, depending on the thickness of the slices. Check the seasoning, turn the heat down and move the liver to a warm dish. Add the juice of 1 lemon to the pan, mixing it with the cooking juices. Add some chopped parsley and pour it over the liver before serving.

Kidneys

After sweetbreads, I like kidneys next best. I particularly like lambs' kidneys. I quite like calves' kidneys, but I prefer to avoid pig and ox kidneys, as they tend to have a stronger taste and are tougher. If you buy whole kidneys, you'll need to cut them in half vertically and remove the stringy white core.

Rognone alla Senape –
KIDNEYS WITH MUSTARD

Here's an old favourite that I used to serve in my restaurant many years ago.

Two calves' livers will serve 4 people, or use 16 lambs' kidneys. Prepare the kidneys by cutting them in half vertically and removing their white cores, then cut the calves' livers into bite-sized pieces. Cook them in a pan on a high heat for about 4 minutes, season them, then set them aside.

Pour 250 ml of cream into the pan and let it reduce on a high heat until it's a golden colour, then add in 2 tablespoons of mustard – I like to use French mustard – and stir it in well. Add the kidneys and stir for few moments before serving.

Rognone con Cipolline –
KIDNEYS WITH SPRING ONIONS

Two calves' livers will serve 4 people, or use 16 lambs' kidneys. Cook the kidneys for about 4 minutes, then add a finely chopped shallot, stirring well. Season, then add 250 ml of cream and bring it to the boil, stirring constantly. Remove the pan from the heat, add 4 sliced spring onions, mix well, then serve.

Desserts

I have always suspected that the great savoury cuisines of the world – Italian, Indian, Thai, Japanese and Chinese – aren't great at desserts. Perhaps palates that are attuned to savoury dishes don't have the same appetite for sweets. It's certainly true that the variety of desserts in Italian restaurants and homes is very limited.

What there is in Italy are large quantities of *pasticcerie*, or pastry shops. Every small town has one, and the display counters will be stuffed with cakes of every kind. There is a long tradition of pastry-making in Italy, going back to the days when Venetian traders started to bring cane sugar from the Orient to Italy in the twelfth century. By the eighteenth and nineteenth centuries, Italian pastry chefs were working in most of the great houses of Europe, including the aristocratic houses of England.

Italians eat a great deal of pastries. People arriving as guests for dinner will turn up with a tray of 10 pastries rather than a bottle of wine. *Pasta sfoglia*, *pasta frolla*, *panforte*, *cannoli*, almond cakes and *panettone* are just some of the different cakes on offer, but pastries like these are the province of professional bakers and are not for this book.

In restaurants, desserts tend to be either some kind of ice cream or a slice of a large cake drenched in liqueur. Occasionally you'll find a *zuppa Inglese*, or an English soup, which is what Italians call a trifle. Sometimes you might find a *Macedonia*, which is nothing more than chopped-up fresh fruits. In fact, fresh fruit is probably the commonest way of ending a meal in Italy.

Still, there are desserts that are distinctively Italian, and few as they may be, we'll cover them now.

Tiramisu – Pick Me Up

I'll begin with *tiramisu* because it's probably the best known of all Italian desserts. Like any recipe that has travelled around the world, it has mutated into dishes far removed from the original, each chef wanting to 'improve' the original. This recipe sticks very closely to what you'd get in most Italian houses.

You will need 250 grams of mascarpone cheese and *savoiardi* biscuits, sometimes sold here under the name 'ladyfingers'. They're light biscuits about the size of a finger and they're traditionally used for *tiramisu*.

Separate 3 eggs and combine the yolks with 200 grams of sugar, half an espresso and a splash of brandy in a bowl. Beat this well, then add the 250 grams of mascarpone, beating until you have a smooth mixture. In a separate bowl, beat the egg whites until stiff, then fold them into the mascarpone mixture.

To assemble the dish, pour the remaining half an espresso into a saucer and dip one side of each ladyfinger in it. Cover the bottom of a serving dish with ladyfingers – the size of the dish will determine if you'll have two or three layers to your *tiramisu*.

Cover the ladyfingers with one-third of the mascarpone mixture, then add more ladyfingers, more mascarpone and more ladyfingers, finishing with a layer of mascarpone. Put it in the fridge for 1 hour before serving.

Zabaglione

There's an easy way to remember this recipe, and it's 4444. To serve 4 people you'll need 4 egg yolks, 4 tablespoons of sugar and 4 fluid ounces of Marsala, which is 120 ml.

Begin by beating the egg yolks with the sugar until the mixture is fluffy, then stir in the Marsala a little at a time while you continue beating.

Put this bowl over a pot of barely simmering water to create a bain-marie and keep stirring until the mixture starts to thicken and rise. Remove it from the heat and pour it into glasses. You can serve it hot as soon as it's made, or you can put it in the fridge and serve it cold.

Granita

Ice creams are beyond the scope of the average kitchen, but a *granita*, or water ice, is not hard to make. All you need is a freezer compartment in your fridge. The principle is simple – you make a coffee or fruit syrup and then you freeze it, stirring occasionally so that it doesn't freeze solid. Between two and a half and three hours is usually enough in a standard freezer. After about an hour and a half, check the *granita* and stir it so that the frozen parts on the outside get mixed in. Then check every 30 minutes or so, each time giving the *granita* another stir.

Granitas are sometimes served as a sorbet between the starter and the main course, when they act as a refresher for the palate. Lemon *granita* is particularly good for this. Otherwise you can serve a *granita* as a palate-cleansing dessert.

Granita al Caffé – COFFEE GRANITA

Make 1 litre of coffee. Percolated coffee is good, but if you use an infuser, make sure you make the coffee strong. Stir in 100 grams of sugar and let it cool before putting it in the freezer. Stir it every half-hour or so. It should be ready to serve in about two and a half hours.

Granita al Limone – LEMON GRANITA

Squeeze enough lemons to make 250 ml of juice, six or seven should be enough. Dissolve 125 grams of sugar in 500 ml of water by bringing it to the boil and stirring for 5 minutes or so to make a syrup.

Let the syrup get cold, then stir in the lemon juice and put it in the freezer. This recipe has a higher proportion of sugar than the coffee *granita*, so it will take about an hour longer to freeze.

Granita di Fragole – STRAWBERRY GRANITA

Push 1 kilo of strawberries through a sieve with a wooden spoon. You should end up with about 500 ml of pulp and juice. Add the juice of half a lemon and half an orange to the strawberry pulp.

Boil 125 ml of water with 125 grams of sugar for 5 minutes or so to make a thick syrup. When the syrup has cooled down, add it to the strawberry pulp and put it in the freezer. It should be ready to serve between 3 and 4 hours later. Raspberry *granita* is made exactly the same way.

Coffee

A meal in Italy will usually end with a coffee, and in Italy that means an espresso unless you specifically ask for a variant. *Lungo*, or long, means with more water than is usual, while *ristretto* is with even less. *Macchiato* means a splash of hot milk, and a *cappuccino* is with plenty of hot milk. A *cappuccino* is considered a food, not a drink. Italians will talk of eating some hot milk for breakfast rather than drinking it, which explains their reaction to people who order a *cappuccino* from lunchtime onwards.

My old friend Dillie Keane visited me in Italy a few times and she quickly became loved by one and all. Her habit of ordering a *cappuccino* at night in the bar caused endless mirth. It became her best-known foible and was much remarked upon. They really viewed this behaviour as perverse and bizarre. Although I would never do it in Italy, I have been known to drink a *cappuccino* in the afternoon here in Ireland – if no Italians can see me.

Until the recent advent of domestic espresso machines, Italians got their espresso fix either in restaurants or in bars. Bars in Italy dispense alcohol like elsewhere, but during the morning they are filled with Italians standing at the counter drinking coffee, tiny cups of strong, black espresso whose smell pervades bar and pavement. This glorious nectar is so rich in flavours and aromas, so redolent of Italy and things Italian, that it still surprises me that there are people who don't like it. Perhaps it is an acquired taste, but once acquired, there are no substitutes. No other coffee comes close to the pure intensity of an espresso.

It came as something of a shock, therefore, to discover that on average, Italians drink less than half the amount of coffee as their northern European neighbours. Perhaps it can be explained by the fact that although morning coffee is virtually a religious rite, few Italians drink more than two a day, and they are, of course, very small cups.

So what makes a *caffè* so special? The answer lies in those wonderful chrome machines that hiss and spit steam. By forcing steam at close to 200°F and at 16 atmospheres of pressure through finely ground coffee, solubles, oils and colloids are carried from the grounds to the cup, giving an espresso its inimitable flavour. A well-made *caffè* will have a golden brown foam on top that should cling to the sides of the cup, which is known as the *crema di caffè*. The steam pressure creates a very different chemical brew to coffee made by infusion techniques. It is concentrated and intense, quite unlike the watery coffee so common here and elsewhere.

How to Make Things for the Larder

These days we leave a lot of food preparation to industry. That's a shame, because not only are we no longer in control of the food we eat, but we're losing the skills that have served mankind for millennia. In this section I want to show you how easy many of these traditional skills are, using only the simplest of equipment that you could find in most kitchens.

Sausages

Of all the things that I've learned to do in a kitchen, nothing has given me more pleasure than making sausages. The effort to enjoyment ratio is satisfyingly good, and if you want to impress your friends, homemade sausage ranks high for sheer rarity value.

There are two kinds of sausage: those that are made to be cooked and eaten right away and those that are intended for keeping, like salami. They are both made the same way. The first thing that you'll need is the casings – the skins that will be stuffed with meat. Most butchers and supermarkets are happy to sell them. Don't be squeamish – they may look like pig guts, but these days they are made from edible cellulose. Buy the widest casing that you can.

The hard part of the operation is getting the meat into the casing. It takes either a little ingenuity or a commercial sausage-making machine. Given the unlikelihood of the second, we'll go with ingenuity. The idea is this: the casing is rolled onto the spout of a funnel like a large prophylactic and a knot is tied in the end. As the meat is pushed down the funnel, it begins to fill the casing, pushing the casing off the spout of the funnel as it fills. If you've got a one-inch diameter casing, ideally you'll need a funnel with a one-inch diameter spout. A Spong mincer with the cutting blades removed can also do the job – I fastened the funnel to the mincer with a Jubilee clip and it worked – but using an electric mincer is a lot less work. I have used a modified silicone tube gun, but now I use a proper sausage-making machine.

The way my granny used to fill the casings was to use a funnel and a wooden spoon. She'd roll the casing onto the funnel spout and fill the funnel with the chopped meat. Then she'd use the handle of the wooden spoon to push the meat through the funnel and into the casing. It works as a system, but you get pockets of air in the sausage. If you're making sausages for air curing, that's a problem, as rot can set in where there's air. She solved this problem by pricking the casing when it was filled with a pin and then carefully squeezed the sausage, which pushed the air out through the pin-pricks.

Assuming an ingenious solution is in place, start with pork sausages. Pork is cheap, so if things go wrong it won't cost much. A casing is about 1.5 metres long and will hold almost 3 kilos of meat. Cheap cuts are good for making sausages, like shoulder or belly. It will look as though there is a lot of fat, but that's only because you can see it. In a standard commercial sausage there's a lot more, you just can't see it because it's dyed and homogenised.

How to Make Sausages

Mincing the meat for the sausages is quick, but not as good as cutting it up small with a sharp knife. You'll retain a better colour to your sausages if you cut the meat rather than mince it.

Cover the bottom of a large mixing bowl with a layer of chopped meat. Sprinkle it with salt, freshly ground black pepper and a little chilli powder. Add another layer of meat and season again. Continue until all the meat is in the bowl and then mix it together well – adding a splash of red wine will make it easier to push into the casing. As you push in the meat, keep a little pressure on the casing so that it won't slide off too quickly. Make sure that it's tightly packed and well filled. When you've done this you'll have a 1.5 metre-long stuffed tube. Take a length of string and gently tie off the tube about 1 centimetre from the starting end – casings do stretch, but a well-filled tube can burst unless you treat it gently. Tie the tube every 10 centimetres or so to make the individual sausages. Hang them up in a dry, airy place for two days.

At this stage you can put them in a fridge or freezer or cook them immediately, slicing them in half lengthways. Done on a griddle, they're a real treat. If you're adventurous, put some aside and weigh them. Hang them up and when they weigh half of the original weight – depending on the temperature and humidity it can take from five days to two weeks – take them down and pack them into a jar, covering them with olive oil. These are salt-cured *salsiccie* or *saucissons secs*; they taste amazing and will keep forever under oil if you can refrain from eating them. When you do eat them, slice them thinly like salami.

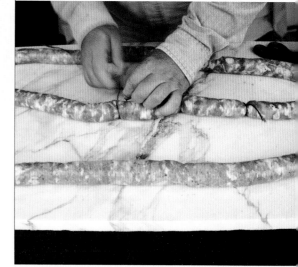

If you can find an easy way to fill the casings, the variety of sausages you can make is bewildering. Some of my favourites include lamb sausages with fresh mint, venison (with one-third pork) and juniper berries, beef sausages and mixed game sausages – your imagination is the only limit.

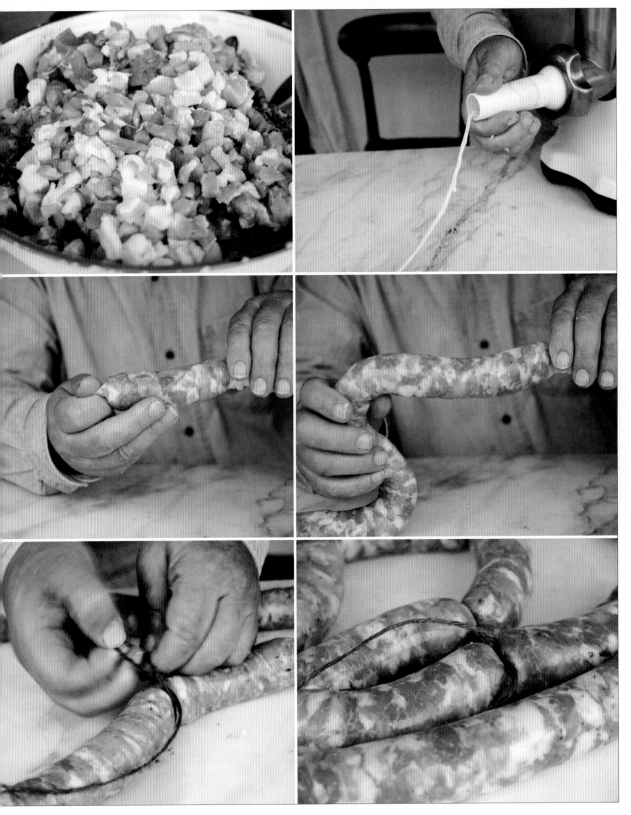

Air-cured Ham

When I think of the centuries of peasant heritage that led to me, I realise that apart from short, stubby fingers, they have bequeathed me a sense of season. Somewhere in my racial subconscious is a deep-rooted feeling that the seasonal cycle is something to respect. I like a world where strawberries are only available in summer, where fruits and vegetables come and go as pointers to the calendar. I'm a traditionalist: I like my foods in season.

And just like a true peasant, I hate waste. Gluts of any foodstuff need careful husbanding – what is not eaten today must somehow be preserved for tomorrow. The age-old methods of preserving food before refrigerators became common were salting, pickling and boiling.

When you think about it, some of the best foods are the result of preserving a glut for later: hard cheeses like cheddar, salami and Parma ham. All over Italy in winter people make hams and sausages for curing because they like the end result, not because they lack fridges. If you're adventurous, let me persuade you to try making your own prosciutto. All you need is an abundance of patience and a leg of pork.

Buy the largest leg of pork that you can and carefully trim away any small tags of meat, leaving the exposed flesh as tidy as possible. Put it in a tray on a bed of coarse salt and cover it completely in salt, taking care to work salt into any crevice, especially around the hipbone and the shank end. Leave it in salt for as many days as it weighs in pounds – 20 days for a 20-pound leg. Salt will draw moisture from the meat, so make sure that the pickle – the moisture that runs out – can drain away. Check it every couple of days and replace any salt that the pickle washes away, concentrating on the hipbone and shank. These are the two areas where rot can set in; salt stops it from happening. You can help remove moisture by pressing the ham – I put a board on top of it and then two concrete blocks on top of that.

This is a race between the salt, which dries the meat, and the bacteria, which thrive in the moist meat, so getting the moisture out is the first goal.

When the time is up, wash off the salt and dry the ham carefully. If you don't have an airy place to hang the ham, use a fan for the first week or two, which really helps the drying process. There's no harm in replacing a little salt around the hipbone and shank for insurance. Try to avoid a draughty place later on, as it will make your ham rock hard in just a couple of months. Check it from time to time; it should be always dry and sweet smelling. Any sign of mould must be wiped with vinegar and any weeping must be treated at once with more salt. If all is well after a month or two, then you've won; you're on the way to a Parma ham.

At this stage you can pretty it up by rubbing olive oil onto the skin, which will give it a lovely golden colour. Rub the exposed meat with olive oil and sprinkle chilli powder over it, working it into any cracks until you have a smooth covering. Apart from making it look nicer and adding a little flavour, it stops the interest of flies during the summer. If your ham has a hip end full of deep crevices, make up a flour and water paste with plenty of salt – two-thirds flour, one-third salt – and push that into the cracks and crevices so that you have a smooth outer surface. The flour and water paste will still allow the ham to dry, and there are no hiding places for insects. If you make your ham in January, you can make your first cuts in October at the earliest.

There is a shortcut that works well but which will not satisfy a purist, although I find it acceptable. A leg of bacon is already salted and costs less than fresh pork. Simply add salt to the hip and shank and proceed as above. I've tried it and it works, though the final taste is never quite the same as using fresh pork. It is, however, a lot simpler.

Once you've mastered this, you might like to try a fancy version that involves removing the bone from the ham before salting. Many commercial hams are made like this in Italy, since they can be sliced easily with an electric slicer. A ham with a bone needs to be sliced by hand.

To do this, lay the ham down with the hipbone facing you. With a sharp knife, cut the whole length of the ham, exposing the bone. Now, as carefully as you can, use the knife to cut all around the bone until you can remove it. When the bone is out, salt the inside and then put it back together. Use a carpet needle and plastic cord to stitch it closed.

If you do it like this you'll definitely need to press the ham with a few concrete blocks or rot will set in where you've removed the bone.

Lastly, to cut a cured ham with a bone, you'll need something to stand it in, or you can slice a finger very easily. You can make a very simple stand out of wood or you can buy one from a specialist shop. Once you've cut into it, you'll have to eat it reasonably quickly – say, over a month or so – because the exposed meat will harden quite fast.

In Italy there's a saying that 'any fool can make a salty ham'. The more salt you use, the less likelihood there is of anything going wrong. The real art and skill is using the bare minimum of salt – just enough to keep rot at bay. This ensures that your ham will taste sweet and not salty.

Cheese

What really distinguishes the modern kitchen from that of rural Ireland a hundred years ago is that we have handed more and more of the kitchen tasks over to industry. There are obvious examples, such as bread, which is now almost totally the preserve of bakeries. Poultry and their eggs are no longer common in gardens; we leave it to large batteries instead. No one keeps a pig any more for bacon and lard. We leave vegetable growing to market gardeners; bottling soft fruit and making jams are becoming rarer. Increasingly we leave the cooking of our food to large industrial concerns.

What troubles me in all this is not its convenience, but rather that the traditional skills, once taken so much for granted, are disappearing. In the rural backwater of Italy that I come from, people still make, grow and preserve much of their own food – although even here, supermarkets and convenience foods are making headway. For years now I have been collecting as many of these ancient skills as I can, since it seems a shame to hand everything over to commercial enterprises. Making flitches of ham, sausages, cheese and pickles may not be something that you'd feel like doing twice a week, but perhaps we should all at least know how it's done.

How to Make Cheese

The EU bureaucrats are doing their best to ensure that you can't buy any foodstuffs that don't come from a large factory. You can no longer legally buy farm eggs, unpasteurised milk or, soon, homemade cakes and jams. Meat can come only from an abattoir and there are varieties of fruit and vegetables that are no longer available for sale. Unless you can do things yourself, you'll soon have no choice but to buy the EU regulation fare in a supermarket.

Even though there are butter mountains and milk lakes, we pay through the nose for cheese. Yet cheese is not hard to make. You may not be able to create a fine Stilton or a runny Brie, but simple cheese is easy. I like to use unpasteurised milk, but it is hard to get unless you live outside the city. You can use supermarket milk, but you'll get much less cheese per litre, as it's already been skimmed of cream.

You can buy rennet in some large chemists. It's what turns milk into curd. Heat the milk to blood heat (roughly 98°F), remove it from the heat and stir in the rennet as directed on the bottle. Cover the pot and leave it to cool. You will find that the milk has become like a jelly. With a long knife, cut the curd in two directions, making cubes roughly 2.5 centimetres square, then cover the pot and leave it. The curds and the whey will separate.

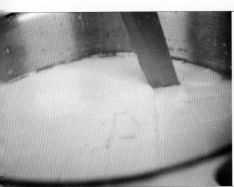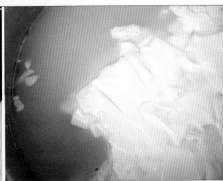

To make a cottage cheese, drain off the whey and drain the curds through cheesecloth. Work salt by hand through the curds and add the herbs of your choice. Push it into a mould and turn it out onto a plate. Keep it in the fridge.

If you want to be cleverer than this and make a long-lasting hard cheese, you must pitch the curds. After they have separated from the whey, leave them in it. Every few hours or so, take a small piece of curd and drop it into a cup of very hot water. If when you take it out it goes stringy, then it's ready. If not, wait a little longer. Depending on the ambient temperature, this could take up to three days. When the curds are pitched, add a small amount of salt and form the cheese in a mould. Put it in an airy place and it will begin to form a hard skin. Turn the cheese every couple of days and occasionally paint the outside with salty water to keep mould at bay. After a month or two you'll have a cheese similar to Pecorino – hard, piquant and good for grating on pasta.

You have another option when the curds are pitched, and that's mozzarella. You'll have noticed that pitched curds go stringy in very hot water – that's the effect we use to make mozzarella. You need very hot water for this and I know people in Italy who can work the curds with their bare hands, but the water is too hot for most people. Instead, use two wooden spoons to work the curds. Gather the stringy curds together by wrapping one spoon around the other, making small balls of cheese. Drop the cheeses into cold brine as you make them. Leave them in brine for a couple of hours and they're ready to eat.

Really fresh mozzarella is virtually unknown in Ireland, but it's a cheese that's at its best when it's very fresh. Try fresh mozzarella once, and you'll no longer be happy with those supermarket offerings.

How to Make Ricotta

When you've finished your cheese-making, you'll be left with whey, the liquid that's left over once you've removed the curds. If you want to store mozzarella, keep back a little whey to store it in. With the remaining whey, you can now make ricotta. Strictly speaking, ricotta isn't cheese, as it's made from the whey, not the curds.

Heat the whey to a gentle simmer, then add an acid, either lemon juice or vinegar. Use 2 tablespoons of acid for 4 litres of whey. Stir this well and the acid will cause the milk solids to precipitate from the whey, making very small particles. Use fine muslin to strain the liquid, and you'll find you have ricotta, which, by the way, means 'twice cooked', because you've heated the liquid twice.

Lightly salt the ricotta and put it in the fridge. It doesn't keep long, so use it as soon as you can. You'll find a lot of recipes in this book that use ricotta.

The Uses of Olive Oil

I'm old enough to remember a time when olive oil in Ireland was something you put in your ear. You bought it in a chemist's in a tiny bottle and it was purely medicinal. Some years ago I introduced an Italian friend of mine, Enzo Mantova, to Ireland and he has since introduced his olive oil here. One of the first things he did was take home a sample of every olive oil he could find that was already on the Irish market. Back at his factory he got his lab technicians to analyse them spectrographically. Most were exactly as you would expect: blends of olive and other vegetable oils. Mentioning no names here for fear of men in wigs, one oil regularly found in tiny medicinal bottles defied analysis. Its spectrographic fingerprint was unmatchable to any known combination of oils.

Today, every supermarket stocks a good range of olive oils – Greek, French, Italian, Spanish and some labelled mysteriously 'produce of the EU'. In real terms, olive oil is cheaper now than it has ever been – a decent extra virgin oil can be bought for about €4 a litre, cheap enough to use it on a daily basis.

Olive oil has many wonderful properties, but it's not great for deep frying since it burns at a lower temperature than other vegetable oils. In these cholesterol-conscious times it can replace butter on vegetables, butter for shallow frying, lard for basting and is essential on a salad. But it also has the property of absorbing flavours, and this makes it ideal for preserving herbs.

Olive Oil for Preserving

In countries where olive oil is a staple, it's also used for preserving things. Once covered in oil and safe from the air, just about anything can be preserved: sardines, salt-cured sausages, cheese, herbs, mushrooms, aubergines and courgettes – these last two are normally sliced and roasted first.

If you've ever grown and dried basil for later use, you'll certainly have been disappointed with the loss of flavour. A good way around this is to put fresh basil – or any other herb – into a jar and cover it with olive oil. Make sure no air bubbles get trapped between the leaves or mould will form. The basil retains more of its flavour, and as a bonus when it's finished, you've got basil-flavoured oil as a treat.

Herb-flavoured Oil

Flavouring olive oil is so simple, you'll wonder why anyone would go out and buy a flavoured oil in a fancy bottle. It's a good idea to keep any interesting bottle that you get – they're always handy for bottling herb oils or even liqueurs.

Fill your fancy bottle with good olive oil and push a sprig of rosemary into the bottle as well as some sliced garlic cloves. Every couple of days, turn the bottle a few times. After two weeks the oil will have already absorbed the flavours. The longer you leave it, the stronger the flavours will become. Experiment with different herbs.

Chilli Oil

You can use this property of flavour absorption to good effect with chillies. I find them difficult to dose when whole, but if you break them up a bit and cover them in a jar with olive oil, then after about three weeks you can use the oil – by now a fiery red – to flavour your food. Dosing it becomes a simple matter of counting teaspoonfuls.

Storing Olive Oil

Olive oil and light don't go well together. If you leave it where light can get it, it can go off. The oil will lose its fresh taste and will start to smell and taste rancid. Keep it in the dark, or keep it in an opaque container.

Sun-dried Tomatoes

Many years ago, my friend Nicola Celestino came back from a holiday in Sicily with a strange variety of dried and spiced fruits which were, he told me, Sicilian specialities. Having tasted my way carefully through them all, it was clear to me that these were acquired tastes – and I was in no hurry to acquire some of them. There was one jar, however, that contained something quite delicious that I was unable to analyse. They were sun-dried tomatoes.

I was so excited at the taste of them that it became a priority to learn how to make them for myself. It turned to be remarkably easy. All you need is sun – three days of it. Even in this country, that's not too hard to find.

Slice plum tomatoes lengthways almost in half, leaving a little on one side so that it opens like a book. Lay them, skin side down, on a large board so that there is a little space between each one. Sprinkle them with salt and leave them exposed to the sun. When they look like shrivelled bats' wings, they're ready. The first year I tried this I made a huge amount – I still had some of that original batch three years later. The reason that they stayed around so long is that I ran out of ideas for what to do with them.

Although they've become an immensely fashionable accessory to the well-laid table and turn up regularly in restaurants in improbable combinations with other foods, they aren't particularly versatile, and once the novelty has worn off they are easily forgotten on the larder shelf. The Sicilians, who have been drying tomatoes for centuries, eat them as a starter, and I think they are right. They are at their best when prepared simply. Here's how.

Try to buy dried tomatoes that are not over-salted. Put them in a jar with a few cloves of garlic and some rosemary. Cover them completely with good olive oil and wait a week or two for all the flavours to blend together. It's as easy as that. Serve them as an *antipasto* with some stuffed olives and perhaps some Parma ham or sliced salami. This simple recipe rekindled my liking for dried tomatoes to such an extent that my once large reserves were quickly depleted.

Pickling

Pickling has been used for millennia as a means of preserving gluts of seasonal foodstuffs. These days we think of it mostly as vegetable pickles, but another word for pickling was 'corning', hence corned beef.

Here is a base recipe for pickle, which you can use for preserving the excess from your garden or simply because it often improves the flavour of foods. I'm not a big fan of cucumber, but if it's sliced and pickled, I'll eat it very happily.

2 litres water

1 litre vinegar

100 grams salt

50 grams sugar

In a medium pot, mix the water, vinegar, salt and sugar. Bring this to the boil to pickle the vegetables of your choice. Five minutes is plenty for sliced cucumber, 15 for dill pickles.

Store your pickles by filling sterilised jars with your chosen vegetable and topping off with the pickle liquid before replacing the caps. You should be able to store things like this for months.

Liqueurs

In Ireland, digestion and bowel movements are conversations we have with doctors; in Italy, these are daily topics of discourse. Italians talk with affection and knowledge about their liver and spleen. I suspect most people in this country would be hard pressed to locate either. Ask an Italian how he feels this morning, and the chances are he'll tell you – in detail.

For a nation of hypochondriacs, a preoccupation with digestion produces some tangible effects. Italy has more pharmacists per capita than any other European country, and they are stuffed not only with all the usual pharmaceuticals, but with aids to digestion. Tablets to take before you go out to eat too much, capsules to help you digest when you have eaten too much and pills to stop you from eating too much. Bars can provide you with an *aperitif* to stimulate your appetite or a *digestivo* to help you cope with that same appetite's results. Don't forget, this is the country that brought you Fernet-Branca.

Since digestion is so much discussed and so well catered for, it's tempting to believe all that you hear about it. I mean, if they spend so much time thinking about it, maybe they know something about it. For instance, they believe that once past the age of 21 we can no longer easily digest everything we throw into our stomachs; raw sweet peppers are a good example. This is where the *digestivo*, the post-prandial liqueur, comes into its own. A good *digestivo* after an enormous meal will have you ready to start again.

The best *digestivo* you can have is a *nocino*, which is based on walnuts. To make your own, first you need alcohol. On the Continent, you can buy 95 per cent ethyl alcohol ready to make into liqueurs in supermarkets. Since most recipes call for alcohol at 50 per cent by volume, you dilute the pure alcohol by half. This means that if you can't get access to pure, neutral alcohol, you'll need to find a comparable spirit. A high-alcohol vodka or perhaps even poitín would do. The more neutral the taste, the better.

If you like the idea of making liqueurs, the base recipe is simple: half a litre of alcohol, half a litre of water, 200 grams of sugar and whatever flavour catches your fancy.

Nocino

Fill a large storage jar with green walnuts – the ones that still have the green outer covering on. Break them open before you put them into the jar and cover them with half a litre of alcohol. Seal the jar and leave it for a month, shaking it every few days. After a month, strain the alcohol from the walnuts. If you've used pure ethyl alcohol, you'll need to add water to it to make it drinkable, so warm half a litre of water and dissolve 200 grams of sugar in it. When it's cool, add it to the strained alcohol. Pour it into sterilised bottles and wait for at least a month before drinking it. The longer you let it stand, the better it will taste.

If you're using a bottle of high-alcohol vodka or poitín, it will already be about 50 per cent alcohol by volume. If you want your liqueur to be reasonably strong, you'll need to dilute your 200 grams of sugar in as little water as possible before adding it to the flavoured alcohol.

Limoncino – LEMON LIQUEUR

Limoncello is made on the Amalfi peninsula and nowhere else. If it's made elsewhere, it has to be called *limoncino*.

Take the rind from 6 large, well-washed lemons, avoiding the bitter pith. It's important to use unsprayed lemons for this, so look for unwaxed organic lemons. Put the lemon peel into a jar and cover it with half a litre of pure ethyl alcohol, vodka or poitín. Give the jar a shake every few days for 21 days. When the time is up, strain the alcohol. Dissolve 200 grams of sugar into half a litre of water if you're using pure ethyl alcohol (or into as little water as possible if using vodka or poitín), add it to the strained alcohol and bottle it. It can be drunk once chilled, but it will improve enormously in flavour over a couple of months.

Coffee Liqueur

This is simple, quick and ready to drink immediately, although like the others it does improve with bottle age.

Make half a litre of strong black coffee and dissolve 200 grams of sugar into it. Add half a litre of alcohol, shake well and refrigerate.

Orange Liqueur – Cointreau Style

You'll need a wide-topped jar big enough to take a large orange easily through the opening. A 2-litre mayonnaise jar is ideal. Pour in half a litre of alcohol. Now comes the fun part. Take a ripe, perfumed orange and thread a string through the middle of it. Hold the string by both ends and lower the orange into the jar until it's about 1 centimetre above the alcohol. Now put the lid on the jar, trapping the string so that the orange remains suspended. Put the jar away for 21 days.

If you watch the jar, you'll notice that a drip will form quite quickly at the bottom of the orange. What's happening is that the alcohol is evaporating inside the jar and is condensing on the skin of the orange, taking a little of the flavour as it does so. The drip will drop into the alcohol and a new drip will form. After three weeks, most of the flavour from the orange peel will now be in the alcohol.

If you've used pure ethyl alcohol, measure out half a litre of water and warm it enough to dissolve 200 grams of sugar in it. Add this to your flavoured alcohol and you have Cointreau. If you've used a bottle of poitín or vodka, use as little water as possible to dilute 150 grams sugar before you add it.

Index